모두가 함께 즐기며 배우는 영어회화!

골든벨 영어퀴즈

모두가 함께 즐기며 배우는 영어회화!

골든벨
영어퀴즈

선형조 지음

Brady Miller 감수

머리말

나는 강남에서 태어나서 잠원동 반원초등학교를 졸업했고, 대치동 대청중학교를 거쳐 지금은 휘문고등학교에 재학 중이다. 나는 지금까지 강남에 살았지만 유학은 둘째 치고 국내 영어 조기교육도 받아본 적이 없다. 천성적으로 나는 노는 것을 좋아하고 공부하기를 너무나 싫어했기 때문에 부모님께서 그냥 편하게 놀게 해 주셨다.

본격적으로 영어공부를 시작한 것은 초등학교 4학년 무렵이었다. 하지만 영어공부를 처음 시작해 보니 친구들과 실력 차이가 너무 벌어져서, 무엇을 어떻게 공부해야 할지 몰라 너무나 막막했다. 영어를 아주 잘하는 많은 친구들에게 질려서 영어에 대한 흥미도 전혀 생기지 않았다. 영어 학원에 가는 것은 지옥 그 자체였다.

그러던 어느 날 영어퀴즈 게임을 접하게 되었다. 영어는 못했지만 상품도 걸려 있었고, 내용이 쉬워 대충 무슨 뜻인지 짐작할 수 있는 문제들이 많아서 내 호기심을 자극했다. 영어퀴즈를 시작한 첫날, 나는 한 문제를 맞힐 수 있었고 거기에 재미를 붙여 영어공부를 시작했다.

영어퀴즈는 어려운 단어도 쉽게 외우게 해주고 단어의 실제 쓰임과 문맥에 대한 이해도를 높여주고 듣기나 회화 실력 향상에도 확실한 효과가 있다. 게다가 영어뿐만 아니라 여러 분야의 다양한 상식을 접할 수 있어 공부하는 보

람이 두 배가 된다. 만약 내가 초등학교 때 영어퀴즈를 접하지 못했더라면 영어를 포기했을 것이다.

이 책을 쓰게 된 동기는 2010년도 휘문고등학교 1학년 2학기 미술 과제물 때문이다. 선생님께서는 무엇이든 원하는 프로젝트 한 가지를 만들어서 제출하라고 하셨다.

나는 친구와 함께 어떤 프로젝트를 선택할까 고민하다가 영어회화 책을 만들어 보기로 했다. 그래서 나의 경험을 살려 이제까지 관심을 갖고 공부해 온 영어퀴즈 문제들을 친구와 함께 정리하고 선별하여 이 책을 펴내게 되었다.

내가 경험했던 것처럼 이 책이 많은 학생들에게 영어를 좋아하게 되는 계기가 되었으면 한다.

2011년 7월 1일
선형조

English Quizzes 골든벨 영어퀴즈

 **Part 1 Geography**

001. What is the highest mountain in the world? / 18
002. What is the highest mountain in South Korea? / 19
003. What is the highest mountain in South and North Korea? / 20
004. What is the longest river in the world? / 21
005. What is the widest river in the world? / 22
006. What is the longest river in South and North Korea? / 23
007. What is the longest river in South Korea? / 24
008. What is the largest country in the world? / 25
009. Which country has the largest population in the world? / 26
010. What is the population of China? / 27
011. What is the deepest ocean in the world? / 28
012. What are the names of all the oceans? / 29
013. What are the names of six continents? / 30
014. What are the three largest nations in North America? / 31
015. What is the capital city of America? / 32
016. In which city can you find the Eiffel Tower? / 33
017. In which city can you find the Statue of Liberty? / 34

Part 2 History

018. Who was the first president of America? / 36
019. Who was the first president of Korea? / 37
020. What was the name of the first kingdom in Korea? / 38
021. In what year did Dangun found Gojoseon? / 39
022. What were the names of the Three Kingdoms of Korea? / 40
023. Who founded each kingdom for the Three Kingdoms in Korea? / 41

024. Who was the first king of the Kingdom of Goryeo? / 42

025. Which king and general of Silla unified the Three Kingdoms of Korea and founded Tongil Silla? / 43

026. What was the capital city of the Kingdom of Goryeo? / 44

027. Who was the founder of Joseon Dynasty? / 45

028. He was the fourth King of Joseon Dynasty. He created the Korean alphabet, Hangul. Who is he? / 46

 Part 3 **Famous Stories**

029. Who is the king of the gods in Greek mythology? / 48

030. Who is the goddess of love and beauty in Greek mythology? / 49

031. Who was famous for being strong in Greek mythology? / 50

032. Who lost his strength when his hair was cut by Delilah? / 51

033. Which book is sold the most in the world? / 52

034. According to the Bible who was Adam's mate? / 53

035. Who received the 10 Commandments from God? / 54

036. What is the fifth commandment of the 10 Commandments? / 55

037. How many books are in the Protestant Bible? / 56

038. What is the first book of the Bible? / 57

039. Who killed Goliath with a slingshot? / 58

040. Who betrayed Jesus by a kiss? / 59

041. When Jesus died on the cross, how old was He? / 60

042. Which Egyptian queen did Caesar fall in love with? / 61

043. What is the name of 'Beauty' in the "Beauty and the Beast"? / 62

044. What are the names of Cinderella's stepsisters? / 63

045. His nose grows longer when he tells a lie. Who is he? / 64

046. Which princess ate the poisoned apple and fell asleep for a long time? / 65

English
Quizzes 골든벨 영어퀴즈

047. What is the name of Hansel's younger sister in a fairy tale? / 66
048. What is the name of Simba's uncle in "The Lion King"? / 67
049. Who is Peter Pan's main enemy? / 68
050. I am part girl and part fish. What am I? / 69
051. What is the name of the mermaid princess and the fish following her in "The Little Mermaid"? / 70
052. What did Jack trade for the beans that created a beanstalk? / 71
053. What did Jean Val-jean steal before he was sentenced to prison for 19 years? / 72
054. What is the name of the author of "Romeo and Juliet"? / 73
055. What are William Shakespeare's four famous tragedies? / 74

 Part 4 **Colors, Plants and Animals**

056. The cars must stop. What color is the traffic light? / 76
057. What color are most grasshoppers? / 77
058. What color is a slice of ripe pineapple? / 78
059. What color do you get when you mix equal amounts of red paint with blue paint? / 79
060. The three traditional primary colors in art are red, yellow and blue. What are the three primary colors of light? / 80
061. I live in a 'hive'. My name rhymes with 'tree'. What am I? / 81
062. I say 'moo'. My name rhymes with 'how'. What am I? / 82
063. I say 'oink'. My name rhymes with 'big'. What am I? / 83
064. How many legs does a spider have? / 84
065. What animals have six legs? / 85
066. What animals have two feet, two wings, a beak and feathers? / 86
067. What kind of animals feeds milk to their young? / 87
068. What does a tadpole grow up to be? / 88
069. What does a caterpillar grow up to be? / 89

070. What did 'the Ugly Duckling' grow up to be? / 90
071. What kind of animals has gills and scales? / 91
072. Which part of a plant makes food for the plant? / 92
073. Which part of a plant makes seeds? / 93
074. Which part of a plant takes in water from the soil? / 94
075. Which part of a plant moves water from the roots to the leaves? / 95

 Part 5 **Body and Shapes**

076. What are your five senses? / 98
077. Which part of your body do you use to taste something? / 99
078. Which part of your body do you use to think? / 100
079. Which organ helps you to breathe? / 101
080. Which organ pumps blood through the body? / 102
081. What shape is a coin? / 103
082. What shape is an egg? / 104
083. What shape has four equal sides and four right angles? / 105
084. What shape has two sets of equal sides and four right angles? / 106
085. What is the formula for calculating the area of a triangle? / 107
086. What shape has five sides and five angles? / 108
087. Which polygon has six sides? / 109

 Part 6 **Numbers and Arithmetic**

088. How many toes do most people have? / 112
089. How many wheels does a tricycle have? / 113
090. A 'dozen' means a group of twelve things. If you have two 'dozen' pencils,

English
Quizzes 골든벨 영어퀴즈

how many pencils do you have? / 114

091. How many players per team play in a professional soccer game? / 115

092. Two teams try to score points by hitting a ball with a bat and running around bases in baseball. How many bases are there in baseball? / 116

093. The U.S. flag is called the Stars and Stripes. How many stars are there on the Stars and Stripes and what do the stars on the American flag stand for? / 117

094. Whose picture is on the US penny? / 118

095. Whose portrait is on the US dime? / 119

096. If you have three quarters, one dime, two nickels and five pennies, how much do you have? / 120

097. What five coins add up to fifty cents? / 121

098. It is a quarter to nine. What time will it be in fifteen minutes? / 122

099. The hour hand on the clock points to six. The minute hand points to 12. What time is it? / 123

100. Two plus three equals five. Five plus five equals ten. Then what is six plus six? / 124

101. Ten minus one equals nine. One hundred minus one equals ninety nine. One thousand minus one equals nine hundred ninety nine. Then what is ten thousand minus one? / 125

102. Twenty five divided by five equals five. Nine divided by three equals three. Then what is one hundred divided by ten? / 126

103. Three multiplied by three equals nine. Ten multiplied by ten equals one hundred. Five multiplied by five equals twenty five. Then what is one hundred multiplied by one hundred? / 127

 Part 7 The Solar System and Languages

104. What is the closest star to the earth? / 130

105. There are eight planets in our solar system. They are Mercury, Venus, Earth, Mars, Jupiter, Saturn, Uranus and Neptune. What is the biggest planet among them? / 131

106. On July 16, 1969, Apollo 11 touched down on the moon. Who was the first astronaut to step on the moon? / 132

107. How do you spell the word that means the opposite of 'boy' ? / 133

108. What is the opposite word of 'polite' ? / 134

109. What does 'U.S.A.' stand for? / 135

110. The synonym of 'big' is 'large'. What is the synonym of 'angry' ? It rhymes with 'dad'. / 136

111. Which country does pizza come from? / 137

112. In the Netherlands, people speak Dutch. In China, Chinese is spoken. What language is spoken in Mexico? / 138

113. Which is more precious, silver or gold? / 139

114. This word means both a part of a tree and a part of an elephant. What is this word? / 140

115. What covers most of the surface of the earth? / 141

116. What bird is the symbol of America? / 142

117. Inside of which shell fish, can you find a pearl? / 143

118. An apple is a fruit. Rice is a grain. Then what is a lettuce? / 144

119. What do you stand on when you weigh yourself? / 145

120. If you are facing north, which direction is on your left? / 146

121. What kind of doctors looks after your teeth? / 147

122. What is the sun made of? / 148

123. What do you call the person who looks after sheep? / 149

124. What date is Christmas? / 150

125. What do you use to get a closer look at the stars? / 151

찾아보기 / 153

English Quizzes

일 러 두 기

이 책에서는 다음과 같은 원칙에 따라 발음을 한글로 표기했다.

- B와 V의 표기: /b=ㅂ/: /v=ㅂ/
- L과 R의 표기: /l=ㄹ/: /r=ㄹ/
- P와 F의 표기: /p=ㅍ/: /f=ㅍ/
- 'r'이 받침으로 쓰이는 경우: car/카ㄹ/
- 모음이 강세를 받지 않을 때 사용되는 부드러운 '어' 발음: /어/
- Th의 된소리 발음: /ⓦ/
- 장모음의 표기: 짧은 /이/ 소리와 비교해 긴 /이-/ 소릿값에 /-/를 첨부해서 표기하였다.
  ex) bee/비-/
- 우리말, 모음 소리 'ㅡ'에 해당하는 영어 소릿값은 없다. 그래서 편의상 'ㅡ' 소리를 표기하기도 하고 때론 생략하기도 했다.
- 그 밖에도 한글 표기 발음기호가 옆으로 기울어져 있을 경우는 부드럽게 발음해야 하는 경우다.

English
Quizzes

모두가 함께 즐기며 배우는 영어회화!

골든벨
영어퀴즈

Part 1

Geography

What is the highest mountain in the world?

- 높은: high/하이/
- 더 높은: higher/하이얼/
- 가장 높은: highest/하이-스트/
- 가장 높은 산: the highest mountain/더 하이-스트 마운튼/
- 세계에서: in the world/인 더 월-르드/

세계에서 가장 높은 산은 무엇일까요?
What is the highest mountain in the world?
/와트 이즈 더 하이-스트 마운튼 인 더 월-르드/

에베레스트 산-Mount Everest/마운트 에버리스트/
* 지명을 묻는 질문에 영어에서는 'Where' 대신에 'What' 을 많이 사용한다.

What is the highest mountain in the world?

The highest mountain in the world is Mount Everest.

What is the highest mountain in South Korea?

- 동: east/이-스트/
- 서: west/웨스트/
- 남: south/사우ㅆ/
- 북: north/노-ㄹㅆ/
- 남한: South Korea/사우ㅆ 커리-어/
- 북한: North Korea/노-ㄹㅆ 커리-어/

남한에서 가장 높은 산은 무엇일까요?
What is the highest mountain in South Korea?
/와트 이ㅈ 더 하이-스트 마운튼 인 사우ㅆ 커리-어/

 Answer

한라산-Mount Halla/마운트 할라/

What is the highest mountain in South Korea?

The highest mountain in South Korea is Mount Halla.

Quiz 003

What is the highest mountain in South and North Korea?

• 남북한: South and North Korea/사우㉛ 앤 ㄷ 노-ㄹ㉛ 커리-어/

남한과 북한에서 가장 높은 산은 무엇일까요?
What is the highest mountain in South and North Korea?
/와트 이ㅈ 더 하이-스트 마운튼 인 사우㉛ 앤 ㄷ 노-ㄹ㉛ 커리-어/

 Answer

백두산-Mount Baekdu/마운트 백두/

What is the highest mountain in South and North Korea?

It is Mount Baekdu.

What is the longest river in the world?

- 긴: long/롱/
- 가장 긴: longest/롱기스트/
- 강: river/리버ㄹ/
- 가장 긴 강: the longest river/더 롱기스트 리버ㄹ/

- 더 긴: longer/롱거ㄹ/
- 길이: length/렝(쓰)/

세계에서 가장 긴 강은 무엇일까요?
What is the longest river in the world?
/와트 이ㅈ 더 롱기스트 리버ㄹ 인 더 월-ㄹ드/

나일 강-The Nile/더 나일/

* 세계에서 가장 긴 강은? 현재 공식 기록으로는 나일 강이 6,650킬로미터로 제일
길다. 하지만 넓이를 포함한 크기에서는 아마존 강이 세계에서 가장 크다. 길이에
서도 어떤 과학자들은 아마존 강의 시작점을 페루 남단에서부터 계산하면 6,800
킬로미터로 세계에서 가장 길다고 주장하고 있다. 남한과 북한에서 가장 긴 강은
압록강이다. 압록강의 길이는 803킬로미터이다. 남한에서는 낙동강이 약 506킬
로미터로 제일 길다.

What is the longest river in the world?

The Nile is the longest river in the world.

What is the widest river in the world?

- 넓은: wide/와이드/
- 더 넓은: wider/와이더 ㄹ/
- 가장 넓은: widest/와이디스트/
- 넓이: width/위ㄷ(쓰)/
- 가장 넓은 강: the widest river/더 와이디스트 리버ㄹ/

세계에서 가장 넓은 강은 무엇일까요?
What is the widest river in the world?
/와트 이ㅈ 더 와이디스트 리버ㄹ 인 더 월-ㄹ드/

아마존 강-The Amazon/디 애머잔/

What is the widest river in the world?

The Amazon is the widest river in the world.

22

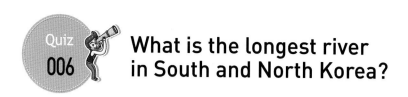

What is the longest river in South and North Korea?

남한과 북한에서 가장 긴 강은 무엇일까요?
What is the longest river in South and North Korea?
/와트 이ㅈ 더 롱기스트 리버ㄹ 인 사우ㅆ 앤ㄷ 노-ㄹㅆ 커리-어/

압록강-The Amnok River/디 암노ㅋ 리버ㄹ/

What is the longest river in South and North Korea?

The Amnok River is the longest river in South and North Korea.

Quiz 007

What is the longest river in South Korea?

남한에서 가장 긴 강은 무엇일까요?
What is the longest river in South Korea?
/와트 이ㅈ 더 롱기스트 *리버ㄹ* 인 사우㉠ *커리-에*/

 Answer

낙동강-The Nakdong River/더 나ㅋ동 *리버ㄹ*/

What is the longest river in South Korea?

The Nakdong River is the longest river in South Korea.

What is the largest country in the world?

- 큰: large/라-ㄹ지/
- 가장 큰: largest/라-ㄹ지스트/
- 나라: country/컨트리/
- 더 큰: larger/라-ㄹ저리/
- 크기: size/사이ㅈ/
- 국가: nation/네이션/
- 세계에서 가장 큰 나라: the largest country in the world
  /더 라-ㄹ지스트 컨트리 인 더 월-ㄹ드/

세계에서 가장 큰 나라는 무엇일까요?
What is the largest country in the world?
/와트 이ㅈ 더 라-ㄹ지스트 컨트리 인 더 월-ㄹ드/

러시아–Russia/러셔/

What is the largest country in the world?

Russia is the largest country in the world.

Which country has the largest population in the world?

- 어느: which/위치/
- 인구: population/파퓰레이션/
- 가장 많은 인구: the largest population

세계에서 어느 나라 인구가 가장 많은가요?
Which country has the largest population in the world?
/위치 컨트리 해즈 더 라-ㄹ지스트 파퓰레이션 인 더 월-ㄹ드/

 Answer

중국-China/차이너/

Which country has the largest population in the world?

China has the largest population in the world.

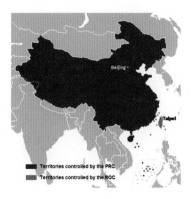

What is the population of China?

- ~의: of/어ㅂ/
- 10억: billion/빌리언/
- 대략: about/어바우ㅌ/
- 중국의 인구: the population of China/더 파퓰레이션 어ㅂ 차이너/

중국의 인구는 얼마나 됩니까?
What is the population of China?
/와ㅌ 이ㅈ 더 파퓰레이션 어ㅂ 차이너/

약 14억 명–about 1.4 billion people
/어바우ㅌ 폴틴 빌리언 피-플/

What is the population of China?

The population of China is about 1.4 billion people.

The five countries with the largest total population

Rank	Country/Territory	Population	Date
1	People's Republic of China	1,338,460,000	July 5, 2010
2	India	1,182,800,000	July 5, 2010
3	United States	309,659,000	July 5, 2010
4	Indonesia	231,369,500	July 5, 2010
5	Brazil	193,152,000	July 5, 2010

Quiz 011

What is the deepest ocean in the world?

- 깊은: deep/디-ㅍ/
- 가장 깊은: deepest/디-피스트/
- 근해: sea/씨-/
- 가장 깊은 대양: the deepest ocean/더 디-피스트 오우션/
- 더 깊은: deeper/디-퍼 ㄹ/
- 깊이: depth/데ㅍ쓰/
- 대양: ocean/오우션/

세계에서 가장 깊은 대양은 무엇입니까?
What is the deepest ocean in the world?
/와트 이즈 더 디-피스트 오우션 인 더 월-ㄹ드/

 Answer

태평양-The Pacific Ocean/더 퍼시피ㅋ 오우션/

What is the deepest ocean in the world?

The Pacific Ocean is the deepest ocean in the world.

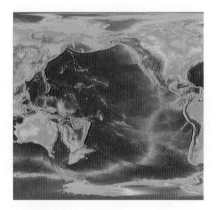

Quiz 012.
What are the names of all the oceans?

- ~의 이름들: the names of/더 네임즈 어브/
- 모든: all/오-르/
- 모든 대양: all the oceans/오-ㄹ 디 오우션즈/
- 모든 대양의 이름: the names of all the oceans
  /더 네임즈 어브 오-ㄹ 디 오우션즈/

모든 대양의 이름은 무엇인가요?
What are the names of all the oceans?
/와트 아르 더 네임즈 *어브* 오-ㄹ 디 오우션즈/

 Answer

태평양–the Pacific/더 퍼시피ㅋ/   대서양–the Atlantic/디 애틀랜틱/
인도양–the Indian/디 인디언/   북극해–the Arctic/디 아르크틱/
남극해–the Southern/더 써던/

What are the names of all the oceans?

The names of all the oceans are; the Pacific, the Atlantic, the Indian, the Arctic and the Southern Oceans.

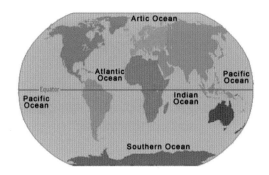

What are the names of six continents?

• 대륙: continent/칸터넌트/

여섯 대륙의 이름은 무엇입니까?
What are the names of six continents?
/와트 아ㄹ 더 네임즈 어ㅂ 씨ㅋ스 칸터넌츠/

 Answer

아시아–Asia/에이저/
유럽–Europe/유러ㅍ/
아프리카–Africa/애프리커/
북아메리카– North America/노–ㄹ⊕ 어메리커/
남아메리카–South America/사우⊕ 어메리커/
오스트레일리아–Australia/오스트 렐리어/
* 여섯 대륙에 남극대륙(Antarctica/앤타ㄹ티커/)을 포함하면 일곱 대륙이 된다.

What are the names of six continents?

The names of six continents are; Asia, Africa, North America, South America, Europe and Australia.

What are the three largest nations in North America?

북아메리카에서 가장 큰 세 나라는 무엇인가요?

What are the three largest nations in North America?

/와트 아ㄹ 더 ㉺리– 라–ㄹ지스트 네이션ㅈ 인 노–ㄹ㉺ 어메리커/

 Answer

캐나다–Canada/캐너더/

멕시코–Mexico/메ㅋ시코우/

미국–The United States of America

/디 유나이티드 스테이츠 어ㅂ 어메리커/

What are the three largest nations in North America?

The three largest nations in North America are the United States of America, Mexico and Canada.

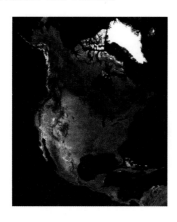

Quiz
015

What is the capital city of America?

- 수도: capital/캐피틀/ = capital city/캐피틀 시티/
- 미국의 수도: the capital city of America/더 캐피틀 시티 어브 어메리커/

미국의 수도는 무엇인가요?
What is the capital city of America?
/와트 이즈 더 캐피틀 시티 어브 어메리커/

 Answer

워싱턴D.C. —Washington D.C/와싱턴 디- 씨-/.

What is the capital city of America?

The capital city of America is Washington D.C.

World Capitals

2007년 기준

Australia	Canberra, 327,700
Brazil	Brasilia, 2,160,100
Canada	Ottawa, Ontario, 1,142,700 (metro. area)
China	Beijing, 10,849,000 (metro. area), 8,689,000 (city proper)
France	Paris, 9,854,000 (metro. area), 2,110,400 (city proper)
Germany	Berlin (capital since Oct. 3, 1990), 3,933,300 (metro. area), 3,274,500 (city proper)
Japan	Tokyo, 35,327,000 (metro. area), 8,483,050 (city proper)
South Korea	Seoul, 10,287,847 (city proper)
Mexico	Mexico City, 19,013,000 (metro. area), 8,591,309 (city proper)
Russia	Moscow, 10,672,000 (metro. area), 10,101,500 (city proper)
Spain	Madrid, 5,130,000 (metro. area), 3,169,400 (city proper)
United Kingdom	London, 7,615,000 (metro. area), 7,429,200 (city proper)
United States	Washington, DC, 570,898

Quiz 016

In which city can you find the Eiffel Tower?

• 에펠탑: the Eiffel Tower/디 아이펄 타워/

어느 도시에서 에펠탑을 찾을 수 있나요?
In which city can you find the Eiffel Tower?
/인 위치 시티 캔 유 파인드 디 아이펄 타워/

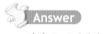

파리-Paris/패리스/

In which city can you find the Eiffel Tower?

The Eiffel Tower is in Paris.

In which city can you find the Statue of Liberty?

• 조각상: statue/스태츄/
• 자유: liberty/리버ㄹ티/
• 자유의 여신상: the Statue of Liberty/스태츄 어ㅂ 리버ㄹ티/

어느 도시에서 자유의 여신상을 찾을 수 있나요?
In which city can you find the Statue of Liberty?
/인 위치 시티 캔 유 파인드 더 스태츄 어ㅂ 리버ㄹ티/

뉴욕-New York/뉴 요ㄹ크/

In which city can you find the Statue of Liberty?

The Statue of Liberty is in New York.

English
Quizzes

모두가 함께 즐기며 배우는 영어회화!

골든벨
영어퀴즈

Part 2
- - - - - - - - - - - -
History

Quiz
018

Who was the first president of America?

- 누구: who/후/
- 대통령: president/프레저던트/
- 미국의 첫 번째 대통령: the first president of America
  /더 퍼르스트 프레저던트 어브 어메리커/

미국의 첫 번째 대통령은 누구였나요?
Who was the first president of America?
/후 워즈 더 퍼르스트 프레저던트 어브 어메리커/

조지 워싱턴-George Washington/조ㄹ지 와싱턴/

Who was the first president of America?

George Washington was the first president of America.

Quiz 019

Who was the first president of Korea?

한국의 첫 번째 대통령은 누구였나요?
Who was the first president of Korea?
/후 워즈 더 퍼르스트 프레저던트 어브 커리-어/

 Answer

이승만–Lee, Seung-man=Seung-man, Lee

Who was the first president of Korea?

Lee, Seung-man was the first president of Korea.

What was the name of the first kingdom in Korea?

• 왕국: kingdom/킹 덤/

한국 최초의 왕국 이름은 무엇인가요?
What was the name of the first kingdom in Korea?
/와ㅌ 이ㅈ 더 네임 어ㅂ 퍼르스트 킹덤 인 커리-어/

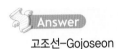

고조선-Gojoseon

What was the name of the first kingdom in Korea?

Gojoseon was the first kingdom in Korea.

Quiz 021 In what year did Dangun found Gojoseon?

- 발견하다, 찾다: find-found-found
- 세우다, 설립하다: found/파운드/–founded/파운디드/–founded/파운디드/

* found는 find(찾다)의 과거형도 되지만 found(설립하다)라는 뜻의 동사 원형도 된다.

단군은 몇 년도에 고조선을 세웠나요?
In what year did Dangun found Gojoseon?
/인 와트 이어ㄹ 디드 단군 파운드 고조선/

Answer

기원전 2333년–2333 B.C./투웬티ⓢ리– ⓢㅓㄹ티ⓢ리– 비– 씨–/

In what year did Dangun found Gojoseon?

Dangun founded Gojoseon in 2333 B.C.

What were the names of the Three Kingdoms of Korea?

• 삼국시대: the Three Kingdoms of Korea

한국 삼국시대의 세 왕국의 이름은 무엇인가요?
What were the names of the Three Kingdoms of Korea?
/와ㅌ 워ㄹ 더 네임ㅈ 어ㅂ 더 ⓢ리- 킹덤ㅈ 어ㅂ 커리-어/

Answer

고구려–Goguryeo　　신라–Silla　　백제–Baekje

What were the names of the Three Kingdoms of Korea?

Goguryeo, Silla and Baekje were the names of the Three Kingdoms of Korea.

Who founded each kingdom for the Three Kingdoms in Korea?

- 각각의: each/이-치/
- 설립했다[설립하다(found)의 과거형]: founded/파운디드/

한국에서 삼국시대의 각 왕국은 누가 세웠나요?
Who founded each kingdom for the Three Kingdoms in Korea?
/후 파운디드 이-치 킹덤 폴 더 ⓦ리- 킹덤즈 인 커리-어/

 Answer

고구려(Goguryeo)-주몽(Jumong)　백제(Baekje)-온조(Onjo)
신라(Silla)-박혁거세(Bak, Hyeokgeose)

Who founded each kingdom for the Three Kingdoms in Korea?

Goguryeo was founded by Jumong, Silla was founded by Bak, Hyeokgeose and Baekje was founded by Onjo.

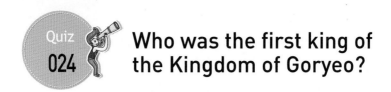

Who was the first king of the Kingdom of Goryeo?

• 고려왕조: the Kingdom of Goryeo /더 킹덤 어브 고려/

고려왕조의 첫 번째 왕은 누구였나요?
Who was the first king of the Kingdom of Goryeo?
/후 워즈 더 퍼르스트 킹 어브 더 킹덤 어브 고려/

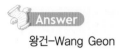

왕건-Wang Geon

Who was the first king of the Kingdom of Goryeo?

Wang Geon was the first king of the Kingdom of Goryeo.

Which king and general of Silla unified the Three Kingdoms of Korea and founded Tongil Silla?

• 통일하다: unify/유니파이/
• 장군: general/제너럴/

삼국을 통일하고 통일신라를 세운 신라의 왕과 장군은 누구인가요?
Which king and general of Silla unified the Three Kingdoms of Korea and founded Tongil Silla?
/위치 킹 앤ㄷ 제너럴 어브 실라 유니파이드 더 ⑅리- 킹덤즈 어브 커리-
어 앤ㄷ 파운디드 통일실라/

신라의 문무왕과 김유신 장군-King Munmu of Silla and General Kim, Yu-shin/킹 문무 어브 실라 앤ㄷ 제너럴 김유신/

Which king and general of Silla unified the Three Kingdoms of Korea and founded Tongil Silla?

King Munmu of Silla and General Kim, Yu-shin unified the Three Kingdoms of Korea and founded Tongil Silla.

What was the capital city of the Kingdom of Goryeo?

고려왕조의 수도는 어디였나요?
What was the capital city of the Kingdom of Goryeo?
/와트 워즈 더 캐피틀 시티 어브 더 킹덤 어브 고려/

송악(=개경=개성)-Songak(=Gaegyeong=Gaesung)

What was the capital city of the Kingdom of Goryeo?

Songak(=Gaegyeong=Gaesung) was the capital city of the Kingdom of Goryeo.

Quiz
027

Who was the founder of Joseon Dynasty?

- 한 가문의 왕조: dynasty/다이너스티/
- 설립자: founder/파운더 ㄹ/
- 조선왕조: Joseon Dynasty

조선왕조를 세운 사람은 누구였나요?
Who was the founder of Joseon Dynasty?
/후 워즈 더 파운더ㄹ 어ㅂ 조선 다이너스티/

이성계–Yi, Seong-gye
* 역사적인 사실을 말할 때는 과거형이나 현재형 모두 가능하다.

Who was the founder of Joseon Dynasty?

Yi, Seong-gye was the founder of Joseon Dynasty.

He was the fourth King of Joseon Dynasty. He created the Korean alphabet, Hangul. Who is he?

- 만들다, 창조하다: create/크리에이트/
- 큰, 위대한: great/그레이트/
- 한글 : the Korean alphabet, Hangul/더 커리언 알파베트 한글/

그는 조선왕조의 네 번째 왕입니다. 그는 한글을 만들었습니다. 그는 누구입니까?
He was the fourth King of Joseon Dynasty. He created the Korean alphabet, Hangul. Who is he?
/히 워즈 더 포ㄹ⑪ 킹 어ㅂ 조선 다이너스티. 히 크리에이티드 더 커리언 알파베트, 한글. 후 이ㅈ 히/

세종대왕-King Sejong the Great/킹 세종 더 그레이트/

He was the fourth King of Joseon Dynasty. He created the Korean alphabet, Hangul. Who is he?

King Sejong the Great was the fourth King of Joseon Dynasty in Korea and he created the Korean alphabet, Hangul.

English
Quizzes

모두가 함께 즐기며 배우는 영어회화!

Part 3

Famous Stories

Quiz 029

Who is the king of the gods in Greek mythology?

- 신: god /갇/
- 그리스의: Greek /그리-ㅋ/
- 신화: mythology /미⊛ㅏㄹ러지/

그리스 신화에서 신들의 왕은 누구인가요?
Who is the king of the gods in Greek mythology?
/후 이ㅈ 더 킹 어ㅂ 더 갇ㅈ 인 그리-ㅋ 미⊛ㅏㄹ러지/

제우스–Zeus /주–스/

Who is the king of the gods in Greek mythology?

Zeus is the king of the gods in Greek mythology.

Quiz 030

Who is the goddess of love and beauty in Greek mythology?

- 여신: goddess/가디스/
- 미: beauty/뷰티/

그리스 신화에서 사랑과 미의 여신은 누구인가요?
Who is the goddess of love and beauty in Greek mythology?
/후 이즈 더 가디스 어브 러브 앤드 뷰티 인 그라ー크 미⚬ㅏ 러러지/

 Answer

아프로디테-Aphrodite/애프러다이티/

Who is the goddess of love and beauty in Greek mythology?

Aphrodite is the goddess of love and beauty in Greek mythology.

Who was famous for being strong in Greek mythology?

- ~로 유명한: be famous for/비 페이머스 포ㄹ/
- ~힘이 세기로 유명한: be famous for being strong/비 페이머스 포ㄹ 비잉 스트롱/

그리스 신화에서 누가 힘이 세기로 유명했나요?
Who was famous for being strong in Greek mythology?
/후 워즈 페이머스 포ㄹ 비잉 스트롱 인 그라ㅡㅋ 미(ㅆ)ㅏ 러러지/

 Answer

헤라클래스–Hercules/허ㄹ큘라ㅡ즈/

Who was famous for being strong in Greek mythology?

Hercules was famous for being strong in Greek mythology.

Who lost his strength when his hair was cut by Delilah?

- 잃다: lose-lost-lost
- 힘: strength/스트렝㉄/
- 성경: Bible/바이블/
- 깎이다: be cut
- 머리를 깎다: get(have) one's hair cut
- 나 머리 깎았다: I got(had) my hair cut/아이 같 마이 헤어ㄹ 커트/
- 데릴라(성경에서 삼손을 배신한 여자): Delilah/딜라일러/

데릴라에게 머리를 깎이자 힘을 잃었던 사람은 누구인가요?
Who lost his strength when his hair was cut by Delilah?
/후 로스트 히스 스트렝㉄ 웬 히스 헤어ㄹ 워즈 커트 바이 딜라일러/

삼손-Samson/샘슨/

Who lost his strength when his hair was cut by Delilah?

Samson lost his strength when his hair was cut by Delilah.

Which book is sold the most in the world?

- 가장(많이), 가장(큰): most/모우ㅅㅌ/
- 가장 많이 팔린: be sold the most/비 소울드 더 모우ㅅㅌ/

세상에서 가장 많이 팔린 책은 어떤 책인가요?
Which book is sold the most in the world?
/위치 부ㅋ 이ㅈ 소울드 더 모우ㅅㅌ 인 더 월-ㄹ드/

 Answer

성경-The Bible/더 바이블/
About 6,000,000,000 copies have been sold. 약 60억 부가 팔렸다.

Which book is sold the most in the world?

- The book which is the most sold in the world is The Bible.

According to the Bible who was Adam's mate?

- ~에 따르면, ~에 의하면: according to~/어코-ㄹ딩 투/
- 아담: Adam/애덤/
- 짝: mate/메이트/
- 이브: Eve/이-ㅂ/

성경에 따르면 아담의 짝은 누구였나요?
According to the Bible who was Adam's mate?
/어코-ㄹ딩 투 더 바이블 후 워즈 애덤즈 메이트/

이브-Eve/이-브/

According to the Bible who was Adam's mate?

Eve was Adam's mate according to the Bible.

Who received the 10 Commandments from God?

- 받다: receive/리시-ㅂ/
- 명령(계명): commandment/커맨드 먼트/
- 십계명: the 10 Commandments/더 텐 커맨드 먼츠/

누가 하나님으로부터 십계명을 받았나요?
Who received the 10 Commandments from God?
/후 리시-브드 더 텐 커맨드먼츠 프럼 갇/

모세-Moses/모우지ㅈ/

Who received the 10 Commandments from God?

Moses received the 10 Commandments from God.

The 10 Commandments
1. Do not have any other god besides the Lord God;
2. Do not have or worship idols (carved images);
3. Do not make wrong use of the name of the Lord your God (or, do not take the name of the Lord in vain);
4. Keep the Sabbath day holy;
5. Honor your mother and your father;
6. Do not commit murder;
7. Do not commit adultery;
8. Do not steal;
9. Do not give false evidence against your neighbor;
10. Do not covet your neighbor's household or lust after your neighbor's spouse.

What is the fifth commandment of the 10 Commandments?

- 다섯 번째 계명: the fifth commandment/더 피프쓰 커맨드먼트/
- 공경하다, 존경하다: honor/아너ㄹ/

십계명 중에서 다섯 번째 계명은 무엇입니까?
What is the fifth commandment of the 10 Commandments?
/와트 이즈 더 피프쓰 커맨드먼트 어브 더 텐 커맨드먼츠/

네 부모를 공경하라–Honor your mother and your father.
/아너ㄹ 유어ㄹ 머더ㄹ 앤드 유어ㄹ 파더ㄹ/

What is the fifth commandment of the 10 Command -ments?

'Honor your mother and your father.' is the fifth commandment.

How many books are in the Protestant Bible?

• 개신교(기독교)의: protestant/프라터스턴트/

개신교의 성경에는 몇 권의 책이 있나요?
How many books are in the Protestant Bible?
/하우 매니 부ㅋㅅ 아ㄹ 인 더 프라터스턴트 바이블/

Answer

66권-66 books(구약은 창세기에서 말라기까지 39권, 신약은 마태복음에서 요한계시록까지 27권 합해서 66권)

＊ 개신교 성경은 66권, 천주교 성경은 74권, 그리스 정교 성경은 79권으로 구성되어 있다.

How many books are in the Protestant Bible?

There are 66 books in the Protestant Bible.

What is the first book of the Bible?

• 기원, 발생, 창시, 성경의 창세기: genesis/제너시ㅅ/

성경의 첫 번째 책은 무엇인가요?
What is the first book of the Bible?
/와ㅌ 이ㅈ 더 퍼ㄹ스트 부ㅋ 어ㅂ 더 바이블/

 Answer

창세기-Genesis/제너시ㅅ/

What is the first book of the Bible?

Genesis is the first book of the Bible.

Who killed Goliath with a slingshot?

- 돌팔매, 새총: slingshot/슬링샤ㅌ/
- 골리앗(성경에 나오는 거인): Goliath/걸라이어ⓢ/

누가 돌팔매로 골리앗을 죽였나요?
Who killed Goliath with a slingshot?
/후 킬드 걸라이어ⓢ 위드 어 슬링샤ㅌ/

다윗-David/데이비드/
* 다윗(이스라엘 2대왕, 성경 시편의 저자)

Who killed Goliath with a slingshot?

David killed Goliath with a slingshot.

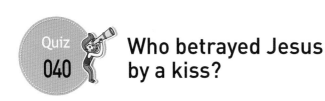

Who betrayed Jesus by a kiss?

- 배신하다: betray /비트레이/
- 입맞춤으로: by a kiss /바이 어 키스/
- 예수: Jesus /지져스/
- 유다: Judas /쥬더스/

누가 입맞춤으로 예수를 배신했나요?
Who betrayed Jesus by a kiss?
/후 비트레이드 지져스 바이 어 키스/

유다-Judas

Who betrayed Jesus by a kiss?

Judas betrayed Jesus by a kiss.

When Jesus died on the cross, how old was He?

- 십자가: cross/크로스/
- 십자가 위에서: on the cross/온 더 크로스/
- 예수의 십자가: the Holy Cross/더 호올리 크로스/
- 죽다: die/다이/ −죽었다: died/다이ㄷ/
- ~때, 언제: when/웬/

예수님께서 십자가 위에서 돌아가셨을 때, 나이는 어떻게 되나요?
When Jesus died on the cross, how old was He?
/웬 지져ㅅ 다이ㄷ 온 더 크로스, 하우 오울드 워즈 히/

Answer

33살−33 years old/ⓦ ㅓㄹ티 ⓦ리 이어ㄹ즈 오울드/

When Jesus died on the cross, how old was He?

Jesus was 33 years old when he died on the cross.

Which Egyptian queen did Caesar fall in love with?

- 이집트의: Egyptian/이짚션/
- ~와 사랑에 빠지다: fall in love with ~/폴 인 러브 위드/
- 시저: Caesar/씨-저러/
- 클레오파트라: Cleopatra/클리어패트러/

시저는 이집트의 어느 여왕과 사랑에 빠졌나요?
Which Egyptian queen did Caesar fall in love with?
/위치 이짚션 퀸 디드 씨-저러 폴 인 러브 위드/

 Answer

클레오파트라–Cleopatra/클리어패트러/

Which Egyptian queen did Caesar fall in love with?

Caesar fell in love with Cleopatra.

Quiz 043

What is the name of 'Beauty' in the "Beauty and the Beast"?

- 짐승: beast/비-스트/
- 미녀, 아름다움: beauty/뷰티/

"미녀와 야수"에서 '미녀'의 이름은 무엇입니까?
What is the name of 'Beauty' in the "Beauty and the Beast"?
/와트 이즈 더 네임 *어브* 뷰티 인 더 뷰티 앤ㄷ 더 비-스트/

 Answer

벨-Belle/벨/
'Belle'은 프랑스어로 '아름답다'라는 뜻이다.

What is the name of 'Beauty' in the "Beauty and the Beast"?

Belle is the name of the 'Beauty' in the story.

What are the names of Cinderella's stepsisters?

- 의붓 자매: stepsister/스테ㅍ시스터ㄹ/
- 신데렐라: Cinderella/신더렐라/
- 재: cinder/신-더ㄹ/

신데렐라의 의붓 자매들의 이름은 무엇입니까?
What are the names of Cinderella's stepsisters?
/와트 아ㄹ 더 네임ㅈ 어ㅂ 신더렐라ㅈ 스테ㅍ시스터ㄹㅈ/

드리젤라와 아나스타샤—Drizella/드리젤라/ and Anastasia/애너스타샤/

What are the names of Cinderella's stepsisters?

Their names are Drizella and Anastasia.

His nose grows longer when he tells a lie. Who is he?

- 더 길어지다: grow longer/그로우 롱거ㄹ/
- 거짓말하다: tell a lie/텔 어 라이/

거짓말을 하면 그의 코는 길어집니다. 그는 누구입니까?
His nose grows longer when he tells a lie. Who is he?
/히스 노우즈 그로우즈 롱거ㄹ 웬 히 텔즈 어 라이. 후 이ㅈ 히/

Answer

피노키오-Pinocchio/피노-키오우/

His nose grows longer when he tells a lie. Who is he?

Pinocchio's nose grows longer when he tells a lie.

Quiz 046

Which princess ate the poisoned apple and fell asleep for a long time?

- 공주: princess/프린세ㅅ/
- 독, 독을 넣다: poison/포이즌/
- 독이 든 사과: the poisoned apple/포이즌드 애플/
- 잠들다: fall asleep/폴 어슬리ㅍ/
- 잠들었다: fell asleep/펠 어슬리ㅍ/
- 오랫동안: for a long time/포ㄹ 어 롱 타임/

어느 공주가 독이 든 사과를 먹고 아주 오랫동안 잠이 들었나요?
Which princess ate the poisoned apple and fell asleep for a long time?
/위치 프린세ㅅ 에이ㅌ 더 포이즌ㄷ 애플 앤ㄷ 펠 어슬리ㅍ 포ㄹ 어 롱타임/

백설공주-Snow White/스노우 와이ㅌ/

Which princess ate the poisoned apple and fell asleep for a long time?

Snow White ate the poisoned apple and fell asleep for a long time.

What is the name of Hansel's younger sister in a fairy tale?

- 동화: fairy tale/페어리 테일/
- 헨젤: Hansel/핸서ㄹ/
- 여동생: younger sister/영거ㄹ 시스터ㄹ/

동화 속에서 헨젤의 여동생 이름은 무엇인가요?
What is the name of Hansel's younger sister in a fairy tale?
/와트 이ㅈ 더 네임 어브 핸서ㄹ즈 영거ㄹ 시스터ㄹ 인 어 페어리 테일/

 Answer

그레텔–Gretel/그레틀/

What is the name of Hansel's younger sister in a fairy tale?

Gretel is the name of Hansel's younger sister.

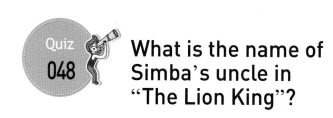

What is the name of Simba's uncle in "The Lion King"?

• 흉터: scar/스카ㄹ/
• 삼촌, 외삼촌, 고모부, 이모부: uncle/엉클/

"라이언 킹"에서 심바의 삼촌 이름은 무엇인가요?
What is the name of Simba's uncle in "The Lion King"?
/와ㅌ 이ㅈ 더 네임 어ㅂ 심바ㅈ 엉클 인 더 라이언 킹/

 Answer

스카-Scar/스카ㄹ/

What is the name of Simba's uncle in "The Lion King"?

Scar is the name of Simba's uncle.

Who is Peter Pan's main enemy?

• 주된: main/메인/
• 적: enemy/에너미/

> 피터팬의 주적(主敵)은 누구입니까?
> Who is Peter Pan's main enemy?
> /후 이ㅈ 피터ㄹ 팬즈 메인 에너미/

후크 선장–Captain Hook/캐ㅍ틴 후ㅋ/

Who is Peter Pan's main enemy?

Captain Hook is Peter Pan's main enemy.

I am part girl and part fish. What am I?

• 부분: part/파 르트/
• 인어: mermaid/멀 메이드/

나는 일부는 소녀이고 일부는 물고기입니다. 나는 무엇일까요?
I am part girl and part fish. What am I?
/아이 앰 파르트 걸ㄹ 앤ㄷ 파르트 피쉬. 와트 앰 아이/

인어-mermaid/멀 메이드/

I am part girl and part fish. What am I?

A mermaid is part girl and part fish.

What is the name of the mermaid princess and the fish following her in "The Little Mermaid"?

- 인어공주: mermaid princess/멀메이드 프린세ㅅ/
- 도다리(바다 물고기), 허둥대다, 허우적거리다: flounder/플라운더ㄹ/

"인어공주"에서 인어공주와 그녀를 따라다니는 물고기 이름은 무엇인가요?
What is the name of the mermaid princess and the fish following her in "The Little Mermaid"?
/와ㅌ 이ㅈ 더 네임ㅈ 어ㅂ 더 멀메이드 프린세ㅅ 앤ㄷ 더 피쉬 팔로윙 헐 인 더 리틀 멀메이드/

 Answer

에리얼과 플라운더-Ariel/에리얼/ and Flounder/플라운더ㄹ/

What is the name of the mermaid princess and the fish following her in "The Little Mermaid"?

The name of the mermaid princess is Ariel and the name of the fish is Flounder.

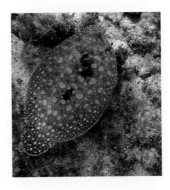

What did Jack trade for the beans that created a beanstalk?

- A와 B를 교환하다: trade A for B /트레이드 에이 포ㄹ 비-/
- 콩: bean /비-ㄴ/
- 창조하다: create /크리에이ㅌ/
- 콩 줄기: beanstalk /비-ㄴ스토ㅋ/

잭은 콩나무(줄기)를 만든 콩을 무엇과 바꿨나요?
What did Jack trade for the beans that created a beanstalk?
/와ㅌ 디ㄷ 재ㅋ 트레/이ㄷ 포ㄹ 더 비-ㄴ즈 대ㅌ 크리에이티ㄷ 어 비-ㄴ스토ㅋ/

Answer

소-cow /카우/

What did Jack trade for the beans that created a beanstalk?

Jack traded a cow for the beans that created a beanstalk.

What did Jean Val-jean steal before he was sentenced to prison for 19 years?

- 훔치다: steal/스티-ㄹ/
- 감옥: prison/프리전/
- (판사가 형량을) 선고하다, 문장: sentence/센텐스/
- 감옥형 선고를 받다: be sentenced to prison/비 센텐스트 투 프리전/

장발장은 무엇을 훔쳐 19년 감옥형을 선고받았나요?
What did Jean Val-jean steal before he was sentenced to prison for 19 years?
/와트 디드 진 발-진 스티-ㄹ 비포 히 워즈 센텐스트 투 프리전 포ㄹ 나인 틴 이어ㄹ즈/

 Answer

빵 한 덩어리-a loaf of bread/어 로우프 어ㅂ 브레드/

What did Jean Val-jean steal before he was sentenced to prison for 19 years?

Jean Val-jean stole a loaf of bread before he was sentenced to prison for 19 years.

What is the name of the author of "Romeo and Juliet"?

• 저자: author/오-ⓦㅓㄹ/

"로미오와 줄리엣"의 저자 이름은 무엇입니까?
What is the name of the author of "Romeo and Juliet"?
/와트 이즈 더 네임 *어브* 디 오-ⓦㅓㄹ *어브* 로우미오우 앤ㄷ 쥴리엣/

Answer

윌리엄 셰익스피어-William Shakespeare/윌리엄 쉐이ㅋ스피*어*ㄹ/

What is the name of the author of "Romeo and Juliet"?

William Shakespeare is the author of "Romeo and Juliet".

Quiz 055

What are William Shakespeare's four famous tragedies?

- 유명한: famous/페이머스/
- 비극: tragedy/트래저디/
- 희극: comedy/카머디/

윌리엄 셰익스피어의 유명한 4대 비극은 무엇입니까?
What are William Shakespeare's four famous tragedies?
/와트 아르 윌리엄 쉐이크스피어즈 포르 페이머스 트래저디즈/

 Answer

햄릿-Hamlet/햄리트/   오셀로-Othello/오-ⓦ ㅔㄹ로우/
맥베스-Macbeth/맥베ⓦ/   리어 왕-King Lear/킹 리어ㄹ/

What are William Shakespeare's four famous tragedies?

Hamlet, Othello, Macbeth and King Lear are Shakespeare's four famous tragedies.

English
Quizzes

모두가 함께 즐기며 배우는 영어회화!

골든벨
영어퀴즈

Part 4

Colors, Plants
and Animals

Quiz 056.

The cars must stop. What color is the traffic light?

- ~해야 한다: must/머스트/
- 교통: traffic/트래피크/
- 빛: light/라이트/
- 교통 신호등: traffic light/트래피크 라이트/
- ★ '~해야만 한다'의 동의어들을 꼭 외워두세요.
  └ must=should=have(has) to=ought to

자동차들이 멈춰야 합니다. 교통 신호등은 무슨 색일까요?
The cars must stop. What color is the traffic light?
/더 카르즈 머스트 스타프. 와트 컬러 이즈 더 트래피크 라이트/

빨간색–Red/레드/

The cars must stop. What color is the traffic light?

The cars have to stop when the traffic light is red.

What color are most grasshoppers?

- 대부분의: most/모우ㅅㅌ/
- 메뚜기: grasshopper/그래스하퍼ㄹ/

대부분의 메뚜기들은 무슨 색인가요?
What color are most grasshoppers?
/와ㅌ 컬러 아ㄹ 모우ㅅㅌ 그래스하퍼ㄹㅈ/

 Answer

녹색-green/그리-ㄴ/

What color are most grasshoppers?

Most grasshoppers are green.

Quiz 058
What color is a slice of ripe pineapple?

- 익은: ripe /라잎/
- 얇게 썰다: slice /슬라이ㅅ/
- 얇게 썬 한 조각: a slice of /어 슬라이ㅅ 어ㅂ/

> 얇게 썬 한 조각의 익은 파인애플은 무슨 색인가요?
> What color is a slice of ripe pineapple?
> /와ㅌ 컬러 이ㅈ 어 슬라이ㅅ *어ㅂ 라잎* 파인애플/

노란색—yellow /옐로우/

What color is a slice of ripe pineapple?

A slice of ripe pineapple is yellow.

78

What color do you get when you mix equal amounts of red paint with blue paint?

- 얻다: get/게트/
- 동등한: equal/이퀄/
- 동등한 양: equal amount

- 섞다: mix/미크스/
- 양: amount/어마운트/
- A와 B를 섞다: mix A with B

같은 양의 빨간색 페인트와 파란색 페인트를 섞으면 어떤 색이 되나요?
What color do you get when you mix equal amounts of red paint with blue paint?
/와트 컬러 두 유 게트 웬 유 미크스 이퀄 어마운츠 어브 레드 페인트 위드 블루 페인트/

보라색–Purple/퍼르플/

What color do you get when you mix equal amounts of red paint with blue paint?

When you mix equal amounts of red paint with blue paint you get the color purple.

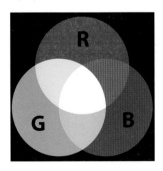

The three traditional primary colors in art are red, yellow and blue. What are the three primary colors of light?

- 미술: art/아르트/
- 전통적인: traditional/트러디셔널/
- 주된, 기본적인: primary/프라이머리/
- 삼원색: the three primary colors/더 리 프라이머리 컬러즈/

미술에서 전통적인 삼원색은 빨강, 파랑, 노랑입니다. 그러면 빛의 삼원색은 무엇일까요?
The three traditional primary colors in art are red, yellow and blue. What are the three primary colors of light?
/더 리 트러디셔널 프라이머리 컬러즈 인 아르트 아르 레드, 옐로우 앤드 블루. 와트 아르 더 리 프라이머리 컬러즈 어브 라이트/

Answer

빨강-red/레드/   파랑-blue/블루/   녹색-green/그리-ㄴ/

The three traditional primary colors in art are red, yellow and blue. What are the three primary colors of light?

The three primary colors of light are red, green and blue.

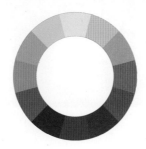

Quiz 061

I live in a 'hive'. My name rhymes with 'tree'. What am I?

- 벌집: hive/하이ㅂ/
- 각운을 이루다: rhyme/라임/

나는 '하이브'에서 살아요. 내 이름은 '트리'와 각운이 맞아요. 나는 무엇일까요?

I live in a 'hive'. My name rhymes with 'tree'. What am I?

/아이 리브 인 어 하이ㅂ. 마이 네임 라임ㅈ 위드 트리-. 와트 앰 아이/

벌-bee/비-/

I live in a hive. My name rhymes with 'tree'. What am I?

A bee lives in a hive and its name rhymes with 'tree'.

I say 'moo'. My name rhymes with 'how'. What am I?

- 소 울음소리 '음매' : moo/무/
- 소(집합적): cattle/캐틀/
- 거세된 수소: ox/아ㅋ스/
- 송아지: calf/캐프/
- 암소: cow/카우/
- 수소(황소): bull/불/

난 '무' 하며 울어요. 내 이름은 '하우' 와 각운이 맞아요. 난 무엇일까요?
I say 'moo'. My name rhymes with 'how'. What am I?
/아이 세이 무. 마이 네임 라임즈 위드 후. 와트 앰 아이/

소(암소)-cow/카우/

I say 'moo'. My name rhymes with 'how'.
What am I?

A cow says 'moo'. Its name rhymes with 'how'.

Quiz 063

I say 'oink'. My name rhymes with 'big'. What am I?

- 돼지 울음소리(꿀꿀): oink/오잉ㅋ/
- 아기 돼지: piglet/피그리ㅌ/
- 돼지(어린 아이들의 말): piggy/피기/ = pig
- 사육 돼지: hog/하ㄱ/
- 돼지(집합적): swine/스와인/
- 돼지 저금통: piggy bank/피기 뱅크/

난 '오잉크'하며 울어요. 내 이름은 '빅'과 각운이 맞아요. 나는 무엇일까요?
I say 'oink'. My name rhymes with 'big'. What am I?
/아이 세이 오잉ㅋ. 마이 네임 *라*임ㅈ 위ㄷ 빅. 와트 앰 아이/

 Answer

돼지-pig/피ㄱ/

I say 'oink'. My name rhymes with 'big'.
What am I?

A pig says 'oink'. Its name rhymes with 'big'.

How many legs does a spider have?

- 다리: leg/레ㄱ/
- 거미: spider/스파이더 ㄹ/

거미의 다리는 몇 개인가요?
How many legs does a spider have?
/하우 매니 레그즈 더즈 어 스파이더ㄹ 해ㅂ/

Answer

여덟 개-Eight/에이ㅌ/

How many legs does a spider have?

A spider has eight legs.

What animals have six legs?

• 곤충: insect/인세ㅋㅌ/

어떤 동물이 여섯 개의 다리를 가지고 있나요?
What animals have six legs?
/와ㅌ 애니멀ㅈ 해ㅂ 씨ㅋ스 레그ㅈ/

곤충-Insect/인세ㅋㅌ/

What animals have six legs?

Insects have six legs.

What animals have two feet, two wings, a beak and feathers?

- 발: foot/푸ㅌ/
- 날개: wing/윙/
- 깃털: feather/페더ㄹ/

- 발들(발의 복수): feet/피-ㅌ/
- 부리: beak/비-ㅋ/

어떤 동물이 두 발과 두 날개, 부리 그리고 깃털을 가지고 있나요?
What animals have two feet, two wings, a beak and feathers?
/와ㅌ 애니멀ㅈ 해ㅂ 투 피-ㅌ, 투 윙ㅈ, 어 비-ㅋ 앤ㄷ 페덜ㅈ/

새-Bird/버ㄹ드/

What animals have two feet, two wings, a beak and feathers?

Birds have two feet, two wings, a beak and feathers.

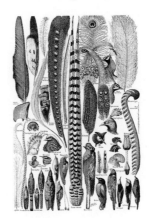

What kind of animals feeds milk to their young?

- 먹이를 주다: feed/피-드/
- 젖을 먹이다: feed milk/피-드 밀ㅋ/
- 종류: kind/카인ㄷ/
- 어떤 종류의: What kind of/와ㅌ 카인ㄷ 어ㅂ/
- 그들의 새끼: their young/데어ㄹ 영/

어떤 종류의 동물이 새끼에게 젖을 먹이나요?
What kind of animals feeds milk to their young?
/와ㅌ 카인ㄷ 어ㅂ 애니멀ㅈ 피-ㄷㅈ 밀ㅋ 투 데어ㄹ 영/

포유류-Mammal/매멀/

What kind of animals feeds milk to their young?

Mammals feed milk to their young.

What does a tadpole grow up to be?

- 자라서 ~가 되다: grow up to be ~/그로우 엎 투 비/
- 올챙이: tadpole/태드포울/

올챙이는 자라서 무엇이 되나요?
What does a tadpole grow up to be?
/와트 더즈 어 태드포울 그로우 엎 투 비/

개구리-Frog/프라ㄱ/

What does a tadpole grow up to be?

A tadpole grows up to be a frog.

What does a caterpillar grow up to be?

- 애벌레: caterpillar/캐터ㄹ필러/
- 나방: moth/모☺/

애벌레는 자라서 무엇이 되나요?
What does a caterpillar grow up to be?
/와트 더즈 어 캐터ㄹ필러 그로우 엎 투 비/

 Answer

나비나 나방-a butterfly or a moth
/어 버터ㄹ플라이 오아ㄹ 어 모☺/

What does a caterpillar grow up to be?

A caterpillar grows up to be a butterfly or a moth.

What did 'the Ugly Duckling' grow up to be?

- 오리: duck/더ㅋ/
- 새끼오리: duckling/더클링/
- '미운 오리 새끼' : 'the Ugly Duckling'
- 백조: swan/스완/

'미운 오리 새끼'는 자라서 무엇이 되었나요?
What did 'the Ugly Duckling' grow up to be?
/와트 디드 더 어글리 더클링 그로우 엎 투 비/

Answer

백조-swan/스완/

What did 'the Ugly Duckling' grow up to be?

'The Ugly Duckling' grew up to be a swan.

What kind of animals has gills and scales?

- 아가미: gill/길/
- 비늘: scale/스케일/

어떤 종류의 동물이 아가미와 비늘을 가지고 있나요?
What kind of animals has gills and scales?
/와트 카인드 어브 애니멀ㅈ 해즈 길ㅈ 앤드 스케일ㅈ/

 Answer

물고기-fish/피쉬/

What kind of animals has gills and scales?

A fish has gills and scales.

Which part of a plant makes food for the plant?

- 잎 하나: a leaf/어 리-프/
- 잎들: leaves/리-브즈/
- 식물: plant/플랜트/

식물의 어느 기관에서 그 식물을 위한 양분을 만드나요?
Which part of a plant makes food for the plant?
/위치 파르트 어ㅂ 어 플랜트 메이ㅋㅅ 푸ㄷ 포ㄹ 더 플랜트/

 Answer

잎-leaf/리-프/

* Parts of a Plant

Roots, a stem, leaves and flowers are the parts of a plant. Roots take in water and minerals from the soil and hold the plant in place. A stem moves water from roots to leaves. It also holds up the plant. Leaves make food for the plant. Flowers make seeds.

Which part of a plant makes food for the plant?

Leaves make food for the plant.

Which part of a plant makes seeds?

• 씨앗: seed/씨-ㄷ/

식물의 어느 기관에서 씨를 만드나요?
Which part of a plant makes seeds?
/위치 파르트 어브 어 플랜트 메이크ㅅ 씨-ㄷㅈ/

꽃-flower/플라우어ㄹ/

Which part of a plant makes seeds?

Flowers make seeds.

Which part of a plant takes in water from the soil?

- 뿌리: root/루트/
- 흡수하다: take in/테이크 인/
- 토양: soil/쏘일/

식물의 어느 기관에서 토양으로부터 물을 흡수하나요?
Which part of a plant takes in water from the soil?
/위치 파르트 어브 어 플랜트 테이크ㅅ 인 워터ㄹ 프럼 더 쏘일/

뿌리—root/루트/

Which part of a plant takes in water from the soil?

Roots take in water from the soil.

Which part of a plant moves water from the roots to the leaves?

- 줄기: stem/스템/
- ~를 옮기다: move/무브/

식물의 어느 기관에서 물을 뿌리에서 잎으로 옮기나요?
Which part of a plant moves water from the roots to the leaves?
/위치 파르트 어브 어 플랜트 무브즈 워터ㄹ 프럼 더 루트츠 투 더 리브즈/

줄기-stem/스템/

Which part of a plant moves water from the roots to the leaves?

The stem moves water from the soil to the leaves.

English
Quizzes

골든벨
영어퀴즈

모두가 함께 즐기며 배우는 영어회화!

Part 5

Body and Shapes

What are your five senses?

- 감각: sense/센스/
- 오감: five senses/파이브 센서즈/

오감에는 무엇이 있나요?
What are your five senses?
/와트 아ㄹ 유어ㄹ 파이브 센서즈/

Answer

시각-sight/싸이트/　　청각-hearing/히어링/　　후각-smell/스멜/
미각-taste/테이스트/　　촉각-touch/터치/

* Your Five Senses

    You have five senses. They are sight, hearing, smell, taste
    and touch. You use your eyes to see, nose to smell, tongue
    to taste, ears to hear and hands to touch.

What are your five senses?

Your five senses are sight, hearing, smell, taste and touch.

Quiz 077

Which part of your body do you use to taste something?

- 혀: tongue/텅/
- 몸, 신체: body/바디/
- 맛을 보다: taste/테이스트/
- 무엇, 어떤 것: something/썸씽/

무엇인가를 맛보기 위해서는 신체의 어느 기관을 사용하나요?
Which part of your body do you use to taste something?
/위치 파ㄹ트 어ㅂ 유어ㄹ 바디 두 유 유우ㅈ 투 테이스트 썸씽/

혀-tongue/텅/

Which part of your body do you use to taste something?

People use their tongue to taste something.

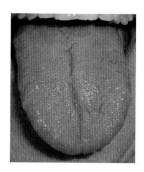

Which part of your body do you use to think?

- 생각하다: think/쌍ㅋ/
- 뇌: brain/브레인/

생각하기 위해서는 신체의 어느 기관을 사용하나요?
Which part of your body do you use to think?
/위치 파ㄹ트 어ㅂ 유어ㄹ 바디 두 유 유우ㅈ 투 쌍ㅋ/

뇌–brain/브레인/

Which part of your body do you use to think?

I use my brain to think.

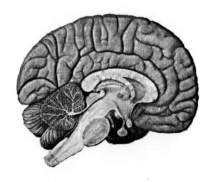

Quiz 079

Which organ helps you to breathe?

- 신체 장기: organ/올건/
- 폐: lung/렁/
- 숨쉬다: breathe/브리드/

어느 장기가 호흡하는 것을 돕나요?
Which organ helps you to breathe?
/위치 올건 헬ㅍㅅ 유 투 브리드/

폐-lung/렁/

Which organ helps you to breathe?

Our lungs help us to breathe.

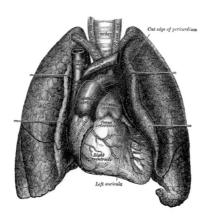

Quiz 080

Which organ pumps blood through the body?

- 펌프질하다: pump/펌프/
- 피: blood/블러ㄷ/
- ~를 통해, 두루두루: through/☺루/
- 심장: heart/하ㄹ트/

어느 장기가 피를 몸 전체로 펌프질해주나요?
Which organ pumps blood through the body?
/위치 올건 펌프ㅅ 블러ㄷ ☺루 더 바디/

 Answer

심장-heart/하ㄹ트/

Which organ pumps blood through the body?

A heart pumps blood through the body.

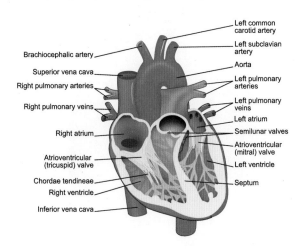

Quiz
081

What shape is a coin?

- 모양: shape/쉐잎/
- 동전: coin/코인/
- 원: circle/Ⓦㅓㄹ클/
- 둥근: round/라운드/

동전은 무슨 모양인가요?
What shape is a coin?
/와트 쉐잎 이ㅈ 어 코인/

원-circle/Ⓦㅓㄹ클/

What shape is a coin?

A coin is round, it has a circular shape.

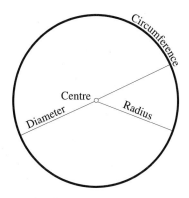

What shape is an egg?

• 타원형, 타원의: oval/오우버ㄹ/

계란은 무슨 모양인가요?
What shape is an egg?
/와ㅌ 쉐잎 이ㅈ 언 에ㄱ/

 Answer

타원형-oval/오우버ㄹ/

What shape is an egg?

It is an oval.

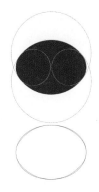

What shape has four equal sides and four right angles?

- 면: side/싸이ㄷ/
- 각: angle/앵글/
- 같은, 동등한: equal/이퀄/
- 직각: right angle/라이ㅌ 앵글/
- 정사각형: square/스퀘어ㄹ/

어떤 모양이 4면의 길이가 같고 4개의 직각을 가지고 있나요?
What shape has four equal sides and four right angles?
/와ㅌ 쉐잎 해ㅈ 포ㄹ 이퀄 싸이ㄷㅈ 앤ㄷ 포ㄹ 라이ㅌ 앵글ㅈ/

 Answer

정사각형–square/스퀘어ㄹ/

What shape has four equal sides and four right angles?

A square has four equal sides and four right angles.

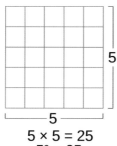

$$5 \times 5 = 25$$
$$5^2 = 25$$

What shape has two sets of equal sides and four right angles?

- 직사각형: rectangle/레ㅋ탱글/
- 길이가 같은 각각의 두 개의 면: two sets of equal sides

어떤 모양이 4면의 길이가 각각 2개씩 같고 4개의 직각을 가지고 있나요?
What shape has two sets of equal sides and four right angles?
/와ㅌ 쉐잎 해ㅈ 포ㄹ 이퀄 싸이ㄷㅈ 앤ㄷ 포ㄹ 라이ㅌ 앵글ㅈ/

직사각형-rectangle/레ㅋ탱글/

What shape has two sets of equal sides and four right angles?

A rectangle has two sets of equal sides and four right angles.

What is the formula for calculating the area of a triangle?

- 공식: formula/포ㄹ뮬러/
- 넓이, 영역: area/에리어/
- 밑변: base/베이스/

- 계산하다: calculate/캘큘레이트/
- 삼각형: triangle/트라이앵글/
- 높이: height/하이트/

삼각형의 넓이를 계산하는 공식은 무엇인가요?
What is the formula for calculating the area of a triangle?
/와트 이즈 더 포ㄹ뮬러 포ㄹ 캘큘레이팅 디 에리어 어ㅂ 어 트라이앵글/

삼각형의 넓이(Area)=밑변의 길이(base)X높이(height)/2

What is the formula for calculating the area of a triangle?

A=b X h /2   (A:Area, b:base, h:height)

Quiz 086

What shape has five sides and five angles?

• 오각형: pentagon/펜태건/

어떤 도형이 5개의 면과 5개의 각을 가지고 있나요?
What shape has five sides and five angles?
/와트 쉐잎 해즈 파이브 싸이드즈 앤드 파이브 앵글즈/

Answer

오각형-pentagon/펜태건/

What shape has five sides and five angles?

A pentagon has five sides and five angles.

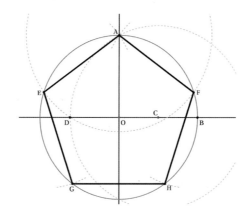

Which polygon has six sides?

- 다각형: polygon/팔리간/
- 육각형: hexagon/헤ㅋ서건/

어떤 다각형이 6개의 면을 가지고 있나요?
Which polygon has six sides?
/위치 팔리간 해ㅈ 씨ㅋㅅ 싸이드ㅈ/

육각형-hexagon/헤ㅋ서건/

Which polygon has six sides?

A hexagon is a polygon with six sides.

English
Quizzes

골든벨
영어퀴즈

모두가 함께 즐기며 배우는 영어회화!

Part 6

Numbers and Arithmetic

How many toes do most people have?

- 발가락: toe/토우/
- 대부분의: most/모우ㅅ트/
- 대부분의 사람들: most people/모우ㅅ트 피플/

대부분의 사람은 몇 개의 발가락을 가지고 있나요?
How many toes do most people have?
/하우 매니 토우ㅈ 두 모우ㅅ트 피플 해ㅂ/

 Answer

열 개-ten/텐/

How many toes do most people have?

Most people have ten toes.

Quiz 089

How many wheels does a tricycle have?

- 바퀴: wheel/위-ㄹ/
- 세발자전거: tricycle/트라이서클/

세발자전거에는 몇 개의 바퀴가 있나요?
How many wheels does a tricycle have?
/하우 매니 위-ㄹㅈ 더ㅈ 어 트라이서클 해ㅂ/

 Answer

세 개-three/(쓰)리-/

How many wheels does a tricycle have?

A tricycle has three wheels.

A 'dozen' means a group of twelve things. If you have two 'dozen' pencils, how many pencils do you have?

- 의미하다: mean/미-ㄴ/
- 12개짜리 묶음: dozen/더즌/
- 연필 한 다스: a dozen pencils/어 더즌 펜설ㅈ/

'더즌'은 12개짜리의 묶음을 의미합니다. 만약 당신이 2 '더즌' 개의 연필을 갖고 있다면 연필은 몇 자루일까요?
A 'dozen' means a group of twelve things. If you have two 'dozen' pencils, how many pencils do you have?
/어 더즌 미-ㄴㅈ 어 그룹 어ㅂ 투웰브 ⑱ㅈ. 이ㅍ 유 해ㅂ 투 더즌 펜설 ㅈ, 하우 매니 펜설ㅈ 두 유 해ㅂ/

 Answer

스물 네 자루-24 pencils/투웬티 포ㄹ 펜설ㅈ/

A 'dozen' means a group of twelve things. If you have two 'dozen' pencils, how many pencils do you have?

If you have two dozen pencils, you have 24 pencils.

Counting Words

dozen=12   score=20(3 score and 10=70)
decade=10년   century=100년
millennium=1,000년

Quiz 091

How many players per team play in a professional soccer game?

- 전문적인, 프로의: professional/프러페셔늘/
- 아마추어의: amateur/애마추어ㄹ/
- ~당, ~마다: per/퍼ㄹ/

프로 축구 경기에서는 팀당 몇 명의 선수가 경기를 하나요?
How many players per team play in a professional soccer game?
/하우 매니 플레이어ㄹ즈 퍼ㄹ 팀 플레이 인 *어* 프러페셔늘 싸커ㄹ 게임/

 Answer

11명-11 players/일레븐 플레이어ㄹ즈/

How many players per team play in a professional soccer game?

Eleven players per team play in a professional soccer game.

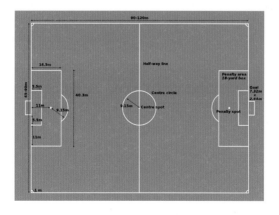

Quiz 092

Two teams try to score points by hitting a ball with a bat and running around bases in baseball.
How many bases are there in baseball?

- 베이스: base/베이스/
- 시도하다: try to/트라이 투/
- 점수를 내다: score point/스코-ㄹ 포인트/
- 점수를 내려고 시도하다: try to score points/트라이 투 스코-ㄹ 포인츠/

야구 경기에서 두 팀이 방망이로 공을 치고 베이스를 돌아 점수를 내려고 합니다. 야구에는 몇 개의 베이스가 있나요?
Two teams try to score points by hitting a ball with a bat and running around bases in baseball. How many bases are there in baseball?
/투 팀-ㅈ 트라이 투 스코-ㄹ 포인트츠 바이 히팅 어 볼 위드 어 뱉 앤드 러닝 어라운드 베이시즈 인 베이스 볼. 하우 매니 베이시즈 아르 데어 ㄹ 인 베이스 볼/

 Answer

네 개—four bases/포ㄹ 베이시ㅅ/.

Two teams try to score points by hitting a ball with a bat and running around bases in baseball. How many bases are there in baseball?

There are four bases in baseball.

The U.S. flag is called the Stars and Stripes. How many stars are there on the Stars and Stripes and what do the stars on the American flag stand for?

- 기, 깃발: flag/플래ㄱ/
- ~라고 불리다: is called/이ㅈ 콜ㄷ/
- 성조기: the Stars and Stripes/더 스타ㄹㅈ 앤ㄷ 스트라잎ㅅ/
- 줄무늬: stripe/스트라잎/
- 상징하다, 의미하다: stand for/스탠ㄷ 포ㄹ/

미국의 국기는 성조기라고 불립니다. 성조기에는 몇 개의 별이 있으며, 별은 무엇을 의미하나요?
The U.S. flag is called the Stars and Stripes. How many stars are there on the Stars and Stripes and what do the stars on the American flag stand for?
/더 유-에ㅅ 플래ㄱ 이ㅈ 콜ㄷ 더 스타ㄹㅈ 앤ㄷ 스트라잎ㅅ. 하우 매니 스타ㄹㅈ 아ㄹ 데어ㄹ 온 더 스타ㄹㅈ 앤ㄷ 스트라잎ㅅ 앤ㄷ 와ㅌ 두 더 스타ㄹㅈ 온 더 어메리칸 플래ㄱ 스탠ㄷ 포ㄹ/

 Answer

50-Fifty/피프티/
50개 별은 미국의 50개의 주(state)를 나타냄.

The U.S. flag is called the Stars and Stripes. How many stars are there on the Stars and Stripes and what do the stars on the American flag stand for?

There are 50 stars on the American flag. The 50 stars represent the 50 states in the United States. The 13 stripes represent the thirteen. original colonies.

Whose picture is on the US penny?

- 누구의: whose/후즈/
- 1센트 동전: penny/페니/

미국의 1센트 동전에는 누구의 그림이 있나요?
Whose picture is on the US penny?
/후즈 피크쳐 이즈 온 더 유-에ㅅ 페니/

 Answer

아브라함 링컨-Abraham Lincoln/에이브러헴 링컨/

Whose picture is on the US penny?

A picture of Abraham Lincoln is on the US penny.

The Coins of United States of America

Penny(1센트)

Nickel(5센트)

Dime(10센트)

Quarter(25센트)

Whose portrait is on the US dime?

- 초상화: portrait/폴트레이트/
- 미국의 10센트 동전: dime/다임/

미국의 10센트 동전에는 누구의 초상화가 있나요?
Whose portrait is on the US dime?
/후즈 폴트레이트 이즈 온 더 유-에ㅅ 다임/

프랭클린 루스벨트–Franklin Roosevelt/프랭클린 로우저벨트/
* 프랭클린 루스벨트는 미국의 32대 대통령이다. 노벨상을 수상한 미국의
27대 대통령 Theodore Roosevelt의 조카로 뉴딜 정책을 도입했다.

Whose portrait is on the US dime?

A portrait of Franklin Roosevelt is on the US dime.

If you have three quarters, one dime, two nickels and five pennies, how much do you have?

- 미국의 25센트 동전: quarter/쿼터 ㄹ/
- 미국의 5센트 동전: nickel/니클/

여러분에게 3개의 quarter와 1개의 dime 그리고 2개의 nickel과 5개의 penny가 있다면 모두 얼마를 가지고 있는 걸까요?
If you have three quarters, one dime, two nickels and five pennies, how much do you have?
/이프 유 해ㅂ ㉠리 쿼터ㄹ즈 원 다임, 투 니클ㅈ 앤ㄷ 파이ㅂ 페니ㅈ, 하우 머치 두유 해ㅂ/

3X25 + 10 + 2X5 + 5 = 100 cents = 1달러

If you have three quarters, one dime, two nickels and five pennies, how much do you have?

You have one dollar.

What five coins add up to fifty cents?

• 동전: coin/코인/
• 합해서 ~가 되다: add up to~/애ㄷ 엎 투/

어떤 동전 5개를 합치면 50센트가 되나요?
What five coins add up to fifty cents?
/와트 파이ㅂ 코인ㅈ 애ㄷ 엎 투 피/프티 센ㅊ/

10센트짜리 동전-dime/다임/

What five coins add up to fifty cents?

Five dimes add up to fifty cents.

It is a quarter to nine. What time will it be in fifteen minutes?

- 15분: a quarter/어 쿼터ㄹ/ = 15 minutes
- 9시 15분 전: a quarter to 9/어 쿼터ㄹ 투 나인/
- 15분 있으면(지나면): in 15 minutes/인 피프틴 미니ㅌㅊ/
- 될까요: will it be/윌 이ㅌ 비/

9시 15분 전입니다. 15분 있으면 몇 시가 될까요?
It is a quarter to nine. What time will it be in fifteen minutes?
/이ㅌ 이ㅈ 어 쿼터ㄹ 투 나인. 와ㅌ 타임 윌 이ㅌ 비 인 피프틴 미니ㅌㅊ/

 Answer

9시-9 o'clock/나인 어클라ㅋ/

It is a quarter to nine. What time will it be in fifteen minutes?

It will be nine o'clock in fifteen minutes.

The hour hand on the clock points to six. The minute hand points to 12. What time is it?

- 시침: hour hand/아우어ㄹ 핸ㄷ/
- 분침: minute hand/미니ㅌ 핸ㄷ/
- ~를 가리키다: point to~/포인ㅌ 투/

시계 위의 시침이 6을 가리키고 있습니다. 분침은 12를 가리키고 있습니다. 몇 시입니까?

The hour hand on the clock points to six. The minute hand points to 12. What time is it?

/더 아우어ㄹ 핸ㄷ 포인ㅌ츠 투 씨ㅋ스. 더 미니ㅌ 핸ㄷ 포인ㅌ츠 투 투웰ㅂ. 와ㅌ 타임 이ㅈ 이ㅌ/

6시-6 o'clock/씨ㅋ스 어클라ㅋ/

The hour hand on the clock points to six. The minute hand points to 12. What time is it?

It is six o'clock.

Two plus three equals five.
Five plus five equals ten.
Then what is six plus six?

- 더하기: plus/플러ㅅ/
- 같다, 동등하다: equal/이퀄/

2 더하기 3은 5입니다. 5 더하기 5는 10입니다. 그러면 6 더하기 6은 얼마
입니까?
Two plus three equals five. Five plus five equals ten. Then what
is six plus six?
/투 플러ㅅ 🎃 리- 이퀄ㅈ 파이ㅂ. 파이ㅂ 플러ㅅ 파이ㅂ 이퀄ㅈ 텐. 덴 와
ㅌ 이ㅈ 씨ㅋㅅ 플러ㅅ 씨ㅋㅅ/

12- twelve/투웰ㅂ/

Two plus three equals five. Five plus five equals ten.
Then what is six plus six?

It is twelve.

Ten minus one equals nine. One hundred minus one equals ninety nine. One thousand minus one equals nine hundred ninety nine. Then what is ten thousand minus one?

- 1백: one hundred/원 헌드러드/
- 1천: one thousand/원 ⓦㅏ우전드/
- 1만: ten thousand/텐 ⓦㅏ우전드/

10 빼기 1은 9입니다. 100 빼기 1은 99입니다. 1,000 빼기 1은 999입니다. 그러면 10,000 빼기 1은 얼마입니까?
Ten minus one equals nine. One hundred minus one equals ninety nine. One thousand minus one equals nine hundred ninety nine. Then what is ten thousand minus one?
/텐 마이너ㅅ 원 이퀄ㅈ 나인. 원 헌드러드 마이너ㅅ 원 이퀄ㅈ 나인티/나인. 원 ⓦㅏ우전드 마이너ㅅ 원 이퀄ㅈ 나인 헌드러드 나인티/ 나인. 덴 와트 이ㅈ 텐 ⓦㅏ우전드 마이너ㅅ 원/

9,999/나인 ⓦㅏ우전드 나인 헌드러드 앤드 나인티/ 나인/

Ten minus one equals nine. One hundred minus one equals ninety nine. One thousand minus one equals nine hundred ninety nine. Then what is ten thousand minus one?

It is nine thousand nine hundred and ninety nine.

Quiz 102

Twenty five divided by five equals five. Nine divided by three equals three. Then what is one hundred divided by ten?

- 나누다: divide/디바이드/
- 나누어지다: be divided/비 디바이디드/
- ~로, ~에 의해: by/바이/

25를 5로 나누면 5입니다. 9를 3으로 나누면 3입니다. 그러면 100을 10으로 나누면 얼마입니까?
Twenty five divided by five equals five. Nine divided by three equals three. Then what is one hundred divided by ten?
/투웬티 파이브 디바이드 바이 파이브 이퀄즈 파이브. 나인 디바이드 바이 ㉺라- 이퀄즈 ㉺라-. 덴 와트 이즈 원 헌드러드 디바이드 바이 텐/

10-ten/텐/

Twenty five divided by five equals five. Nine divided by three equals three. Then what is one hundred divided by ten?

It is ten.

Three multiplied by three equals nine. Ten multiplied by ten equals one hundred. Five multiplied by five equals twenty five. Then what is one hundred multiplied by one hundred?

- 곱하다:multiply/멀티플라이/
- 곱해지다: be multiplied/비 멀티플라이드/

3에 3을 곱하면 9입니다. 10에 10을 곱하면 100입니다. 5에 5를 곱하면 25입니다. 그러면 100에 100을 곱하면 얼마입니까?
Three multiplied by three equals nine. Ten multiplied by ten equals one hundred. Five multiplied by five equals twenty five. Then what is one hundred multiplied by one hundred?
/ⓒ 리- 멀티플라이드 바이 ⓒ 리- 이퀄ㅈ 나인. 텐 멀티플라이드 바이 텐 이퀄ㅈ 원 헌드러드. 파이ㅂ 멀티플라이드 바이 파이ㅂ 이퀄ㅈ 투웬티/파이ㅂ. 덴 와트 이ㅈ 원 헌드러드 멀티플라이드 바이 원 헌드러드/

 Answer

1만-ten thousand/텐 ⓒ ㅏ 우전드/

Three multiplied by three equals nine. Ten multiplied by ten equals one hundred. Five multiplied by five equals twenty five. Then what is one hundred multiplied by one hundred?

It is ten thousand.

English
Quizzes

모두가 함께 즐기며 배우는 영어회화!

골든벨
영어퀴즈

Part 7

The Solar System and Languages

Quiz 104

What is the closest star to the earth?

- 가까운: close/클로ㅅ/
- 더 가까운: closer/클로서ㄹ/
- 가장 가까운 closest/클로지스트/

지구와 가장 가까운 별은 무엇인가요?
What is the closest star to the earth?
/와ㅌ 이ㅈ 더 클로지스ㅌ 스타ㄹ 투 디 어ㄹ⊛/

태양-the sun/더 썬/
* Our Solar System
  The Sun is a closest star to the earth.
  There are eight planets which move around the Sun.
  Their names are Mercury, Venus, Earth, Mars, Jupiter, Saturn,
  Uranus and Neptune. The biggest planet in our solar system
  is Jupiter. Jupiter is 1,400 times bigger than Earth in volume.
  It has eight moons.

What is the closest star to the earth?

The sun is the closest star to the earth.

There are eight planets in our solar system.
They are Mercury, Venus, Earth, Mars, Jupiter, Saturn, Uranus and Neptune.
What is the biggest planet among them?

- 행성: planet/플래니ㅌ/
- 수성: Mercury/머ㄹ큐리/
- 지구: Earth/어ㄹ☺/
- 목성: Jupiter/주퍼터ㄹ/
- 천왕성: Uranus/유러너ㅅ/

- 태양계: solar system/쏠러ㄹ 시스템/
- 금성: Venus/비너ㅅ/
- 화성: Mars/마ㄹㅈ/
- 토성: Saturn/쌔턴/
- 해왕성: Neptune/네ㅍ툰/

우리 태양계에는 8개의 행성이 있습니다. 그것은 수성, 금성, 지구, 화성, 목성, 토성, 천왕성, 해왕성입니다. 이 중 가장 큰 행성은 무엇인가요?
There are eight planets in our solar system. They are Mercury, Venus, Earth, Mars, Jupiter, Saturn, Uranus and Neptune. What is the biggest planet among them?
/데어ㄹ 아ㄹ 에이ㅌ 플래니ㅌㅅ 인 아우어ㄹ 쏠-러ㄹ 시스템. 데이 아ㄹ 머ㄹ큐리, 비너ㅅ, 어ㄹ☺, 마ㄹㅈ, 주퍼터ㄹ, 쌔턴, 유러너ㅅ 앤ㄷ 네ㅍ툰 와ㅌ 이ㅈ 더 비기스ㅌ 플래니ㅌ 어망 뎀/

 Answer

목성-Jupiter/주퍼터ㄹ/

There are eight planets in our solar system. They are Mercury, Venus, Earth, Mars, Jupiter, Saturn, Uranus and Neptune. What is the biggest planet among them?

Jupiter is the biggest planet in our solar system.

Quiz 106

On July 16, 1969, Apollo 11 touched down on the moon. Who was the first astronaut to step on the moon?

- 착륙하다: touch down/터치 다운/
- 우주비행사: astronaut/애스트러나트/

1969년 7월 16일에 아폴로 11호가 달에 착륙했습니다. 달에 처음으로 발을 디딘 우주 비행사는 누구였나요?
On July 16, 1969, Apollo 11 touched down on the moon. Who was the first astronaut to step on the moon?
/온 줄라이 씨ㅋ스틴 나인틴씨ㅋ스티/나인 어폴로 일레븐 터치ㅌ 다운 온 더 문. 후 워ㅈ 더 퍼르스ㅌ 애스트러나ㅌ 투 스테ㅍ 온 더 문/

 Answer

닐 암스트롱–Neil Armstrong/니-ㄹ 아ㄹㅁ 스트롱/

On July 16, 1969, Apollo 11 touched down on the moon. Who was the first astronaut to step on the moon?

Neil Armstrong was the first astronaut to set foot on the moon.

How do you spell the word that means the opposite of 'boy'?

- 의미하다: mean /미-ㄴ/
- 철자를 말하다: spell /스펠/
- ~는 철자가 어떻게 되나요? : How do you spell ~ /하우 두 유 스펠/

'boy' 의 반대를 뜻하는 단어의 철자는 어떻게 되나요?
How do you spell the word that means the opposite of 'boy'?
/하우 두 유 스펠 더 워ㄹ드 대ㅌ 민-ㅈ 디 아퍼지ㅌ 어ㅂ 보이/

Answer

소녀-g-i-r-l /걸ㄹ/
The opposite of 'big' is 'small'. The opposite of 'male' is 'female'. The opposite of 'long' is 'short'. The opposite of 'handsome' is 'ugly'. The opposite of 'cheap' is 'expensive'. The opposite of 'teacher' is 'student'.

How do you spell the word that means the opposite of 'boy'?

It is a 'g-i-r-l'.

What is the opposite word of 'polite'?

- 예의 바른: polite/펄라이트/
- 불손한: rude/루ㄷ/ = impolite/임펄라이트/

'polite' 의 반대말은 무엇인가요?
What is the opposite word of 'polite'?
/와ㅌ 이ㅈ 디 아퍼지ㅌ 워ㄹ드 어ㅂ 펄라이트/

 Answer

impolite/임펄라이트/ or rude/루ㄷ/

What is the opposite word of 'polite'?

It is 'impolite' or 'rude'.

What does 'U.S.A.' stand for?

• 나타내다, 상징하다, 대표하다: stand for/스탠드 포르/

'U.S.A.' 는 무엇을 나타내나요?
What does 'U.S.A.' stand for?
/와트 더즈 유우 에스 에이 스탠드 포르/

 Answer

U.S.A.는 United States of America를 나타낸다.

What does 'U.S.A.' stand for?

It stands for United States of America.

* 참고

What does 'V.I.P.' stand for?

It stands for 'very important person'.

Quiz

110

The synonym of 'big' is 'large'. What is the synonym of 'angry'? It rhymes with 'dad'.

• 동의어: synonym/씨노님/

'big'의 동의어는 'large'입니다. 'angry'의 동의어는 무엇인가요? 그것은 'dad'와 각운이 맞아요.
The synonym of 'big' is 'large'. What is the synonym of 'angry'? It rhymes with 'dad'.
/더 씨노님 어브 빅 이즈 라르지. 와트 이즈 씨노님 어브 앵그리. 이트 라임 즈 위드 대드/

화난-mad/매드/

The synonym of 'big' is 'large'. What is the synonym of 'angry'? It rhymes with 'dad'.

The synonym of angry is 'mad'. 'Mad' rhymes with 'dad'.

Which country does pizza come from?

- ~ 출신이다, ~나온다: come from/컴 프럼/
- 피자: pizza/피-ㅌ서/

피자는 어느 나라에서 유래된 음식인가요?
Which country does pizza come from?
/위치 컨츄리 더ㅈ 피-ㅌ서 컴 프럼/

이탈리아-Italy/이털리/

Which country does pizza come from?

Pizza comes from Italy.

In the Netherlands, people speak Dutch. In China, Chinese is spoken. What language is spoken in Mexico?

- 네덜란드어, 네덜란드의: Dutch/더치/
- 말해진다: is spoken/이즈 스포-큰/
- 중국어, 중국의: Chinese/차이니ス/

네덜란드에서는 네덜란드어를 씁니다. 중국에서는 중국어를 사용합니다. 그러면 멕시코에서는 어떤 언어를 사용하나요?
In the Netherlands, people speak Dutch. In China, Chinese is spoken. What language is spoken in Mexico?
/인 더 네덜런ㄷス 피-플 스피-ㅋ 더치. 인 차이너 차이니ス 이즈 스포-큰. 와트 랭귀지 이즈 스포-큰 인 메ㅋ시코우

스페인어Spanish/스패니쉬/

In the Netherlands, people speak Dutch. In China, Chinese is spoken. What language is spoken in Mexico?

Spanish is spoken in Mexico.

Which is more precious, silver or gold?

- 금: gold/고울ㄷ/
- 은: silver/씰버ㄹ/
- 귀중한, 값비싼: precious/프레셔ㅅ/

금과 은 중에서 어느 것이 더 귀중한가요?
Which is more precious, silver or gold?
/위치 이즈 모-ㄹ 프레셔ㅅ, 씰버ㄹ 오-ㄹ 고울ㄷ/

 Answer

금-Gold/고울ㄷ/

Which is more precious, silver or gold?

Gold is more precious than silver.

This word means both a part of a tree and a part of an elephant.
What is this word?

- ~의 한 부분: a part of/어 파르트 어브/
- 코끼리의 코, 나무의 몸통: trunk/트렁크/
- A와 B 둘 다: both A and B/보ⓦ 에이 앤ㄷ 비-/

이 단어는 나무의 한 부분과 코끼리의 한 부분, 둘 다를 의미합니다. 이 단어는 무엇일까요?
This word means both a part of a tree and a part of an elephant. What is this word?
/디ㅅ 워ㄹ드 미-ㄴㅈ 보ⓦ 어 파르트 어브 어 트리 앤ㄷ 어 파르트 어브 언 엘러펀트. 와ㅌ 이ㅈ 디ㅅ 워ㄹ드/

트렁크-trunk/트렁크/

This word means both a part of a tree and a part of an elephant. What is this word?

It is 'trunk'.

Quiz 115

What covers most of the surface of the earth?

- 덮다, 덮개: cover/커버ㄹ/
- 표면: surface/써ㄹ퍼ㅅ/

지구 표면의 대부분을 덮고 있는 것은 무엇입니까?
What covers most of the surface of the earth?
/와ㅌ 커버ㄹㅈ 모우스ㅌ 어ㅂ 더 써ㄹ퍼ㅅ 어ㅂ 디 어ㄹ㉛/

물−water/워터ㄹ/

What covers most of the surface of the earth?

Water covers most of the surface of the earth.

Quiz 116

What bird is the symbol of America?

- 상징: symbol/씸벌/
- 대머리의: bald/보-ㄹㄷ/

> 미국을 상징하는 새는 무엇입니까?
> What bird is the symbol of America?
> /와ㅌ 버ㄹ드 이ㅈ 더 씸벌 *어ㅂ 어메리커*/

 Answer

대머리 독수리-bald eagle/보-ㄹㄷ 이-글/

What bird is the symbol of America?

The bald eagle is the symbol of America.

Inside of which shell fish, can you find a pearl?

- ~안에: inside/인사이ㄷ/
- 조개류, 갑각류: shellfish/쉘피쉬/
- 진주: pearl/펄ㄹ/
- 굴: oyster/오이스터ㄹ/

어느 어패류에서 진주를 찾을 수 있나요?
Inside of which shell fish, can you find a pearl?
/인사이ㄷ 어ㅂ 위치 쉘 피쉬 캔 유 파인ㄷ 어 펄ㄹ/

 Answer

진주조개-pearl oyster/펄ㄹ 오이스터ㄹ/

Inside of which shell fish, can you find a pearl?

You can find a pearl inside of a pearl oyster.

An apple is a fruit. Rice is a grain. Then what is a lettuce?

- 과일: fruit/프루트/
- 쌀: rice/라이스/
- 상추: lettuce/레터스/

사과는 과일입니다. 쌀은 곡물입니다. 그러면 상추는 무엇일까요?
An apple is a fruit. Rice is a grain. Then what is a lettuce?
/언 애플 이즈 어 프루트. 라이스 이즈 어 그레인. 덴 와트 이즈 어 레터스/

 Answer

채소, 야채-vegetable/베지터블/

An apple is a fruit. Rice is a grain. Then what is a lettuce?

It is a vegetable.

Quiz 119

What do you stand on when you weigh yourself?

- 무게를 재다, 무게가 나가다: weigh/웨이/
- 무게: weight/웨이ㅌ/

몸무게를 잴 때는 무엇 위에 서나요?
What do you stand on when you weigh yourself?
/와ㅌ 두 유 스탠ㄷ 온 웬 유 웨이 유어ㄹ셀프/

 Answer

저울-scale/스케일/

What do you stand on when you weigh yourself?

You stand on a scale when you weigh yourself.

Quiz 120

If you are facing north, which direction is on your left?

• ~를 향하다, 마주보다: face/페이스/
• 방향: direction/디 렉션/

당신이 북쪽을 향하고 있다면 당신의 왼쪽은 어떤 방향입니까?
If you are facing north, which direction is on your left?
/이프 유 아ㄹ 페이싱 노ㄹ㉠, 위치 디레ㅋ션 이ㅈ 온 유어ㄹ 레프트/

 Answer

서쪽-west/웨스트/

If you are facing north, which direction is on your left?

The west is to your left.

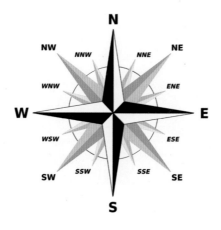

Quiz 121

What kind of doctors looks after your teeth?

• 돌보다: look after/루ㅋ 애프터/ = take care of

어떤 의사가 당신의 치아를 돌보나요?
What kind of doctors looks after your teeth?
/와트 카인ㄷ 어ㅂ 다ㅋ터ㄹㅈ 루ㅋ 애프터 유어ㄹ 티-㊪/

치과의사-dentist/덴티스트/

What kind of doctors looks after your teeth?

Dentists look after your teeth.

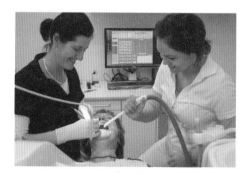

What is the sun made of?

• ~으로 만들어진: be made of/비 메이ㄷ 어ㅂ/

태양은 무엇으로 만들어져 있나요?
What is the sun made of?
/와ㅌ 이ㅈ 더 썬 메이ㄷ 어ㅂ/

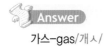

가스–gas/개ㅅ/

What is the sun made of?

It is made of gas.

Quiz 123

What do you call the person who looks after sheep?

• A를 B라고 부르다: call A B

양을 돌보는 사람을 뭐라고 부르나요?
What do you call the person who looks after sheep?
/와ㅌ 두 유 콜 더 퍼ㄹ선 후 루ㅋㅅ 애프터 쉬-ㅍ/

 Answer

양치기-shepherd/쉐퍼ㄹ드/

What do you call the person who looks after sheep?

The person who looks after sheep is a shepherd.

149

What date is Christmas?

크리스마스는 몇 월 며칠인가요?
What date is Christmas?
/와트 데이트 이즈 크리스머스/

12월 25일–December 25/디셈버 트웨티파이브/

What date is Christmas?

It is December 25.

What do you use to get a closer look at the stars?

Quiz 125

• ~를 자세히 보다: get a closer look at~/게ㅌ 어 클로우서ㄹ 루ㅋ 에ㅌ/

별들을 자세히 보기 위해 무엇을 사용하나요?
What do you use to get a closer look at the stars?
/와ㅌ 두 유 유우ㅈ 투 게ㅌ 어 클로우서ㄹ 루ㅋ 에ㅌ 더 스타ㄹㅈ/

망원경-telescope/텔리스코우ㅍ/

What do you use to get a closer look at the stars?

You use a telescope.

English
Quizzes

모두가 함께 즐기며 배우는 영어회화!

골든벨
영어퀴즈

찾아보기

찾아보기

A

단어	문제번호
about: 대략	010
according to~:	
~에 따르면, ~에 의하면	034
Adam: 아담	034
a dozen pencils: 연필 한 다스	090
Africa: 아프리카	013
a leaf: 나뭇잎	072
all: 모든	012
all the oceans: 모든 대양	012
a loaf of bread: 빵 한 덩어리	053
amateur: 아마추어(의)	091
amount: 양	059
angle: 각	083
angry: 화난	110
Antarctica: 남극대륙	013
a part of: ~의 한 부분	114
Aphrodite: 아프로디테	030
a quarter: 4분의 1	098
a quarter to 9: 9시 15분 전	098
area: 면적, 지역	085
art: 미술, 예술	060
Asia: 아시아	013
a slice of: 얇게 썬 한 조각	058
astronaut: 우주비행사	106
Australia: 오스트레일리아, 호주	013
author: 저자	054

B

단어	문제번호
bald: 대머리의	116
bald eagle: 대머리 독수리	116
base: 야구의 루, 베이스	092
base: 밑변	085
beak: 부리	066
bean: 콩	052
beanstalk: 콩 줄기	052
beast: 짐승	043
beauty: 미녀, 아름다움	030, 043
be cut: 깎이다	032
be divided: 나누어지다	102
be famous for being strong:	
힘이 세기로 유명한	031
be made of~: ~으로 만들어진	122
be sold the most:	
가장 많이 팔린	033
be multiplied: 곱해지다	103
be sentenced to prison:	
감옥형 선고를 받다	053
betray: 배신하다	040
Bible: 성경	032

billion: 10억   **010**

blood: 피   **080**

body: 몸, 신체   **077**

both A and B: A와 B 둘 다   **114**

brain: 뇌   **078**

breathe: 숨쉬다   **079**

bull: 수소(황소)   **062**

by: ~로, ~에 의해   **102**

by a kiss: 입맞춤으로   **040**

C

단어	문제번호

call A B: A를 B라고 부르다   **123**

Caesar: 시저   **042**

calculate: 계산하다   **085**

calf: 송아지   **062**

Canada: 캐나다   **014**

capital: 수도=capital city   **015**

Captain Hook: 후크 선장   **049**

cattle: 소   **062**

China: 중국   **009**

Chinese: 중국어, 중국의   **112**

cinder: 재   **044**

Cinderella: 신데렐라   **044**

circle: 원   **081**

Cleopatra: 클레오파트라   **042**

close: 가까운   **104**

closer: 더 가까운   **104**

closest: 가장 가까운   **104**

coin: 동전   **081, 097**

come from: ~출신이다, ~나온다   **111**

comedy: 희극   **055**

commandment: 명령   **035**

continent: 대륙   **013**

country: 나라   **008**

cover: 덮다, 덮개   **115**

cow: 소(암소)   **052, 062**

create: 만들다, 창조하다   **028, 052**

cross: 십자가   **041**

D

단어	문제번호

David: 다윗
(이스라엘 2대왕 성경 시편의 저자)   **039**

date: 날짜   **124**

deep: 깊은   **011**

deeper: 더 깊은   **011**

deepest: 가장 깊은   **011**

Delilah: 데릴라   **032**

dentist: 치과의사   **121**

골든벨
영어퀴즈

찾아보기

depth: 깊이　011
die: 죽다　041
dime: 10센트 동전　097
direction: 방향, 지시　120
divide: 나누다　102
dozen: 12개짜리 묶음　090
duck: 오리　070
duckling: 새끼오리　070
Dutch: 네널란드어, 네덜란드의　112
dynasty: 한 가문의 왕조　027

E

단어	문제번호
each: 각각의	023
Earth: 지구	105
east: 동쪽(의)	002
enemy: 적	049
equal: 동등한, 같은	059, 083, 100
equal amount: 동등한 양	059
Europe: 유럽	013

F

단어	문제번호
face: ~를 향하다, 마주보다	120
fairy tale: 동화	047
fall asleep: 잠들다	046
famous: 유명한	055
feather: 깃털	066
feed: 먹이를 주다	067
feed milk: 젖을 먹이다	067
feet: 발들(발의 복수)	066
fifty: 50	093
find: 발견하다, 찾다	021
five senses: 오감	076
flag: 기, 깃발	093
flounder: 도다리(바다 물고기), 허둥대다, 허우적거리다	051
flower: 꽃	073
foot: 발	066
for a long time: 오랫동안	046
formula: 공식	085
found-founded-founded: 세우다, 설립하다	021
founder: 설립자	027
Franklin Roosevelt: 프랭클린 루스벨트	095
fruit: 과일	118

G

단어	문제번호
gas: 가스	122
general: 장군	025
get: 얻다	059
get a closer look at~: ~를 자세히 보다	125
get(have) one's hair cut: 머리를 깎다	032
gill: 아가미	071
god: 신	029
goddess: 여신	030
Goguryeo: 고구려	023
gold: 금	113
Goliath: 골리앗(성경에 나오는 거인)	039
grasshopper: 메뚜기	057
great: 큰, 위대한	028
green: 녹색	057, 060
Greek: 그리스의	029
grow longer: 더 길어지다	045

H

단어	문제번호
Hamlet: 햄릿	055
hearing: 청각	076
heart: 심장	080
height: 높이	085
Hercules: 헤라클레스	031
high: 높은	001
higher: 더 높은	001
highest: 가장 높은	001
hive: 벌집	061
honor: 공경하다, 존경하다	036
hour hand: 시침	099

I

단어	문제번호
impolite: 불손한	108
insect: 곤충	065
inside: ~안에	117
in the world: 세계에서	001
is called: ~라고 불리다	093
is spoken: 말해진다	112

J

단어	문제번호
Jesus: 예수	040
Joseon Dynasty: 조선왕조	027
Judas: 유다(성경에서 예수를 판 사람)	040
Jupiter: 목성	105

length: 길이	004
lettuce: 상추	118
liberty: 자유	017
long: 긴	004
longer: 더 긴	004
longest: 가장 긴	004
look after: 돌보다	121
lung: 폐	079

K

단어	문제번호
kind: 종류, 친절한	067
kingdom: 왕국	020
King Lear: 리어왕	055
King Sejong the Great: 세종대왕	028

L

단어	문제번호
large: 큰	008
larger: 더 큰	008
largest: 가장 큰	008
leg: 다리	064

M

단어	문제번호
Macbeth: 맥베스	055
mad: 화난	110
main: 주된	049
mammal: 포유류	067
Mars: 화성	105
mean: 의미하다	090, 107
Mercury: 수성	105
mermaid: 인어	050
mermaid princess: 인어공주	051
Mexico: 멕시코	014
minute hand: 분침	099
mix: 섞다	059
mix A with B: A와 B를 섞다	059

Mount Everest: 에베레스트 산 · · · · · · · 001
Mount Halla: 한라산 · · · · · · · 002
Mount Baekdu: 백두산 · · · · · · · 003
most: 대부분의 · · · · · · · 057, 088
most people: 대부분의 사람들 · · · · · · · 088
moth: 나방 · · · · · · · 069
move: ~를 옮기다 · · · · · · · 075
multiply: 곱하다 · · · · · · · 103
must: ~해야 한다 · · · · · · · 056

N

단어	문제번호

nation: 국가 · · · · · · · 008
Neptune: 해왕성 · · · · · · · 105
New York: 뉴욕 · · · · · · · 017
nickel: 미국의 5센트 동전 · · · · · · · 096
north: 북쪽 · · · · · · · 002
North America: 북아메리카 · · · · · · · 013
North Korea: 북한 · · · · · · · 002

O

단어	문제번호

ocean: 대양 · · · · · · · 011
of: ~의 · · · · · · · 010
oink: 꿀꿀(돼지 울음소리) · · · · · · · 063
one hundred: 1백 · · · · · · · 101
one thousand: 1천 · · · · · · · 101
Onjo: 온조 · · · · · · · 023
on the cross: 십자가 위에서 · · · · · · · 041
organ: 신체 장기 · · · · · · · 079
Othello: 오셀로 · · · · · · · 055
oval: 타원형의, 타원의 · · · · · · · 082
ox: 거세된 수소 · · · · · · · 062
oyster: 굴 · · · · · · · 117

P

단어	문제번호

Paris: 파리 · · · · · · · 016
part: 부분 · · · · · · · 050
pearl: 진주 · · · · · · · 117
pearl oyster: 진주조개 · · · · · · · 117
pentagon: 오각형 · · · · · · · 086
per: ~당, ~마다 · · · · · · · 091
pig: 돼지 · · · · · · · 063

골든벨
영어퀴즈

찾아보기

piggy:
돼지(어린 아이들의 말)=pig   063

piggy bank: 돼지 저금통   063

piglet: 아기 돼지   063

Pinocchio: 피노키오   045

pizza: 피자   111

planet: 행성   105

plus: 더하기   100

point to~: ~를 가리키다   099

poison: 독, 독을 넣다   046

polite: 예의 바른   108

polygon: 다각형   087

population: 인구   009

portrait: 초상화   095

precious: 귀중한, 값비싼   113

president: 대통령   018

primary: 주된, 기본적인   060

princess: 공주   046

prison: 감옥   053

professional: 전문의, 프로의   091

protestant: 개신교(기독교)의   037

pump: 펌프질하다   080

purple: 보라색   059

Q

단어	문제번호
quarter: 미국의 25센트 동전	096

R

단어	문제번호
receive: 받다	035
rectangle: 직사각형	084
rhyme: 각운을 이루다	061
rice: 쌀	118
ripe: 익은	058
right angle: 직각	083
river: 강	004
root: 뿌리	074
round: 둥근	161
rude: 무례한	108
Russia: 러시아	008

S

단어	문제번호
Samson: 삼손	032
Saturn: 토성	105
scale: 저울	119

scale: 비늘 071

scar: 흉터 048

score point: 점수를 내다 092

sea: 근해 011

seed: 씨앗 073

sense: 감각 076

sentence:
(판사가 형량을) 선고하다, 문장 053

shepherd: 양치기 123

side: 면 083

Silla: 신라 022

silver: 은 113

sight: 시각 076

size: 크기 008

slice: 얇게 썰다 058

slingshot: 돌팔매, 새총 039

smell: 후각 076

Snow White: 백설공주 046

soil: 토양 074

solar system: 태양계 105

something: 무엇, 어떤 것 077

south: 남쪽 002

South America: 남아메리카 013

South and North Korea:
남한과 북한 003

South Korea: 남한 002

spell: 철자를 말하다 107

spider: 거미 064

square: 정사각형 083

statue: 조각상 017

stand for: 상징하다, 의미하다 093

steal: 훔치다 053

stem: 줄기 075

strength: 힘 032

stepsister: 의붓 자매 044

stripe: 줄무늬 093

surface: 표면 115

swan: 백조 070

swine: 돼지(집합적) 063

symbol: 상징 116

synonym: 동의어 110

단어	문제번호

take in: 흡수하다 074

taste: 맛을 보다, 미각 076, 077

telescope: 망원경 125

ten thousand: 1만 101

관사 the가 붙은 구문(문제번호순)

the highest mountain:
가장 높은 산 001

the Nile: 나일 강 004

골든벨 영어퀴즈

찾아보기

the widest river: 가장 넓은 강 005

the Amazon: 아마존 강 005

the Amnok River: 압록강 006

the Nakdong River: 낙동강 007

the largest country in the world:

세계에서 가장 큰 나라 008

the largest population:

가장 많은 인구 009

the population of China:

중국의 인구 010

the pacific: 태평양 010

the names of all the oceans:

모든 대양들의 이름 012

the Atlantic: 대서양 012

the Indian: 인도양 012

the Artic: 북극해 012

the southern: 남극해 012

the United States of America: 미국 014

the capital city of America :

미국의 수도 015

the Effel Tower: 에펠탑 016

the Statue of Liberty:

자유의 여신상 017

the first president of America:

미국의 첫 번째 대통령 018

the Three Kingdoms of Korea:

삼국시대 022

the Kingdom of Goryeo:

고려왕조 024

the Korean alphabet, Hangul:

한글 028

the Bible 성경 033

the 10 Commandments:

10계명 035

the fifth commandment:

다섯 번째 계명 036

the Holy Cross: 예수의 십자가 041

the States and Stripes: 성조기 041

the closest star: 가장 가까운 별 104

the sun: 태양 104

the Ugly Duckling:

미운 오리 새끼 070

think: 생각하다 **078**

three: 세 개 **089**

through: ~를 통해 **080**

toe: 발가락 **088**

tongue: 혀 **077**

touch: 촉각, 만지다 **076**

touch down: 착륙하다 **106**

traditional: 전통적인 **060**

triangle: 삼각형 **085**

tricycle: 세발자전거 **089**

trunk: 코끼리의 코, 나무의 몸통   114
try to: 시도하다   092
try to score points:
점수를 내려고 시도하다   092
two sets of equal side:
길이가 같은 각각의 두 개의 면   084

U

단어	문제번호

uncle: 삼촌, 외삼촌, 고모부   048
unify: 통일하다   025
Uranus: 천왕성   105

V

단어	문제번호

vegetable: 야채   118
Venus: 금성   105

W

단어	문제번호

Wan Geon: 왕건   024

water: 물   115
weigh:
무게를 재다, 무게가 나가다   119
weight: 무게   119
west: 서쪽   002
what kind of: ~어떤 종류의   067
when: ~때, 언제   041
which: 어느   009
who: 누구   018
wide: 넓은   005
wider: 더 넓은   005
widest: 가장 넓은   005
width: 넓이   005
wing: 날개   066

Y

단어	문제번호

Yi, Seong-gye: 이성계   027
younger sister: 여동생   047

Z

단어	문제번호

Zeus: 제우스   029

모두가 함께 즐기며 배우는 영어회화!

골든벨 영어퀴즈

2011년 7월 15일 초판 1쇄 인쇄
2011년 7월 21일 초판 1쇄 발행

지은이 | 선형조

펴낸이 | 김영철
펴낸곳 | 국민출판사
등록 | 제6-0515호
주소 | 서울특별시 마포구 서교동 382-14
전화 | (02)322-2434 (대표) 팩스 | (02)322-2083
홈페이지 | www.kukminpub.com

편집 | 최용환 · 양승순 · 김옥남
디자인 | 서정희   본문디자인 | 홍수미
영업 | 김종헌 · 이민욱   관리 | 한정숙